Armando Marsans

Armando Marsans

A Cuban Pioneer in the Major Leagues

PETER T. TOOT

McFarland & Company, Inc., Publishers
Jefferson, North Carolina, and London

LIBRARY OF CONGRESS CATALOGUING-IN-PUBLICATION DATA

Toot, Peter T., 1969–
    Armando Marsans : a Cuban pioneer in the major
leagues / Peter T. Toot.
        p.   cm.
    Includes bibliographical references and index.

    ISBN 0-7864-1584-3 (softcover : 50# alkaline paper)

    1. Marsans, Armando, 1887–1960.   2. Baseball players—
Cuba—Biography.   3. Baseball Players—United States—
Biography.   I. Title.
    GV865.M3463T66   2004
    796.357'092—dc22   2003017943

British Library cataloguing data are available

Cover photograph: Armando Marsans *(National Baseball Hall of
Fame Library, Cooperstown, N.Y.)*

Manufactured in the United States of America

*McFarland & Company, Inc., Publishers
    Box 611, Jefferson, North Carolina 28640
    www.mcfarlandpub.com*

To all those whose love of baseball
keeps our game, and its history, alive

Acknowledgments

My family and friends head the long list of people whose knowledge, generosity, and support made this book possible. My mother and Tony Wilkins were frequent and good critics of this work. My siblings, Alex and Betsy Timken, were supportive, perhaps without knowing it. John Alderman, Alex Walley, and Erin Matias helped with their interest, questions, and suggestions. Jennifer Dewey is responsible for having guided me through moments of self-doubt that were potentially fatal for this book; she gave me the confidence to finish. Eric Evers deserves thanks for his work, and so does Allegra Huston. Jerome Bernstein's sage advice allowed me to understand who I am and to be patient through the writing process. I hope the many people who helped me in some way that I have not mentioned will please accept my gratitude and my apology for not mentioning them by name.

I also would like to acknowledge the librarians who patiently pointed me in the correct direction. Tim Wiles and the amazing staff of the Baseball Hall of Fame's Giammatti Research Library deserve special mention, as does the staff in the Connecticut State Library's microfilm division.

Contents

x Contents

Preface

Several different ideas for books about Armando Marsans's life arose as I came to know him through my research: What Marsans meant to a young post-colonial Cuba; Marsans's life as Greek tragedy in which a young man develops exceptional skill and with it hubris, for which the gods punish him by depriving him of the game he loves, then allow him to return to baseball but without his extraordinary skills. Each of these aspects of Armando's life is worthy of a complete work, but it was how Americans reacted to Marsans that most intrigued me.

Marsans's journey through our culture, as a star in white baseball, as one of the first Latino celebrities in the United States, and as a player in the Negro Leagues, allowed him to intimately experience our society's views of ethnicity. What he saw in nearly twenty seasons in the United States was a young, powerful country struggling to find an identity in its new ethnic makeup.

Racial prejudice was prevalent in Marsans's era. African-Americans had been emancipated from slavery only fifty years before Marsans first played in the major leagues, and they continued to be the victims of racism that frequently manifested itself in violent acts. The people of the United States saw Latinos, whether immigrants or living in their native countries, as inferior. These views were frequently based on stereotypes informed by such events as the Spanish-American War and the Mexican Revolution.

This book—part sociological study, part biography—gives the reader a glimpse of the United States, and the stereotypes it held about Latinos, as seen in the journey of a complex man through a microcosm of our culture, what Bart Giamatti called a "great and glorious game"[1]: Baseball.

1

Homecoming

An early autumn sun of 1912 sank out of the Caribbean sky toward the Gulf of Mexico as a crowd of Cubans awaited the ship that brought their hero home. His arrival had been scheduled for four o'clock in the afternoon. It was now six. Cuba's sporting fans waited with excitement, murmuring the name "Marsans." The fans' dedication was made more impressive by the fact they had also waited at the docks the previous day, mistakenly believing their hero was due to arrive then.

Many of the men stood on shore scanning the horizon. Others cruised the water in launches hoping to be the first to see their hero's ship. The few women in the crowd gravitated to one another, their parasols and large hats forming islands in the sea of Edwardian suits.

Someone spotted a small, dark shape on the horizon. Word passed quickly: it must be the *Mascotte*. Smokestacks materialized atop the shape as the form became distinct. The big ship finally entered Havana harbor. Armando Marsans stood at the rail waving to the crowd. Olive skin, darkened by a summer playing baseball, stretched tightly over his high, prominent cheekbones. Black hair and heavy eyebrows added weight to his face. Marsans wore the smile of the celebrated, but, as always, his eyes were what drew one's attention. Even on this joyful day, there was an intensity in his dark irises that spoke of the promise of success.

The *Mascotte* dropped anchor and doctors boarded the ship to inspect the passengers and crew, attempting to prevent disease from entering Cuba. When the doctors cleared the ship, Marsans boarded a tugboat that transferred him to the wharf with the other passengers. He limped ashore to the applause of his worshippers, making his way through a long line of admirers and photographers.

Marsans's five-foot-ten-inch, 157-pound frame was taut even in its injured state. He wore a three-piece suit with a vest buttoned high on his chest, exposing little of the shirt that closed around his neck in a high, starched, white collar circled by a dark bow tie. Marsans exuded athleticism, moving with fluidity despite his injury. Marsans's two brothers, Mario and Raul, greeted him. After posing for photographs for the newspapers, Marsans hastily shook a few hands and climbed into a car with his brothers. Armando Marsans, the new hero of a new nation, hurried home to see his mother.

Armando Marsans returned to Cuba from his first full season in the National League crowned with laurels. The twenty-four-year-old Cuban was a sensation playing for the Cincinnati Reds in the 1912 season. He batted .314 and stole thirty-five bases in one hundred and ten games, playing primarily as an outfielder. Leading Cuban newspapers of the day sent correspondents to follow the man who was being called the best all-around player to enter the major leagues since "Shoeless" Joe Jackson.[1]

Marsans's abilities perfectly suited the game of baseball as it was played in the first decades of the 20th century. Before Babe Ruth revolutionized the game with power, a premium was placed on speed in what is now known as the "Deadball Era." Some baseball historians believe the baseball was softer in that time and did not fly off the bat the way it does today. Home runs were a rarity and large ballparks allowed for many extra base hits. Heinie Zimmermann of the Chicago Cubs led the National League in home runs in 1912 with a total of fourteen. (In the 2001 season, Barry Bonds set the all-time home run record with 73.)

Soon after his return to Cuba, Marsans's countrymen honored him in a ceremony at Havana's City Hall. Just before 2 o'clock on October 17th, 1912, Marsans and Augustín Parla, the first Cuban to receive a pilot's license in a time of crazed fascination with flying, made their way to City Hall. "The mere announcement that

Marsans was to go to City Hall to receive the medal was the cause of a great throng to fill the immediate vicinity of the City Hall and to crowd the chamber where the ceremony of delivering the medals was to be held."[2]

With a band playing and people cheering, Marsans and Parla entered the building. Family members and dignitaries from the city escorted them to the designated chamber. The President of the Municipal Government and the Mayor each spoke, lauding Marsans and Parla in the ceremony. The city presented each man with a parchment document and a solid gold medal with the seal of Havana on one side and an inscription on the other. Marsans's medal read "From the Municipal Government to the notable Cuban baseball player, Armando Marsans." Marsans and Parla walked out into the Cuban sun, the crowned heroes of a new country.

In the autumn of 1912 Cuba was a young republic. She had shed her colonial status fourteen years earlier, with the help of the United States, in the Spanish-American War. Cuba's sports heroes were Ramon Fonst, winner of gold medals in fencing in the 1900 and 1904 Olympic Games; Alfredo de Oro, the world champion in billiards; and the great Cuban chess player, Jose Raúl Capablanca. It was baseball, however, that fascinated the island's sporting public. A Cuban excelling in the National League signified that Cuba's athletes could compete on any playing field in the world. More importantly, it was an allegory of Cuba's emergence as a fully-fledged nation.

The first documented accounts of a bat and ball in Cuba date from 1864, when three young students returned from the United States with the implements of baseball in their trunks and its rules in their minds. The game's early development in Cuba is lost to history, but Cubans have chosen December 27, 1874, the date of the first recorded game on the island, as the celebrated beginning of baseball in their country.

The history of baseball in Cuba in the 19th century is inextricably tied to the Cuban elite. Unlike the game's development within the middle and lower classes in the United States, it was the Cuban upper classes, exposed to baseball while in the U.S., who spread the game throughout their country. In his definitive history of Cuban baseball, *The Pride of Havana*, Professor Roberto González Echevarría describes the game's significance this way:

In the Cuba of the 1880s, particularly in Havana and cities such
as Matanzas, baseball was part of a host of social activities for
mostly young middle- to upper-class men and women. These
activities were part of the "decadent" spirit of the *belle epoque*,
decadent here meaning something useless and frivolous, the
opposite of work and worship. Decadent activities involved primarily the body as a means of obtaining both pleasure and
health. They were leisurely, collective, lucid activities, often taking place outdoors. They were also occasions to wear colorful
attire, including, in this case, the baseball uniforms, to
exchange presents and prizes, and to indulge in vaguely erotic
play, such as dancing... These rituals were animated by an artistic spirit that celebrated the exotic, the foreign, the artificial,
and the erotic.[3]

Baseball attracted both sexes, with many women attending
games as spectators and thereby discovering a new opportunity to
move in the public sphere of Cuban culture.[4] The games and their
associated social activities were venues for Cuban women to interact
with one another and with the opposite sex. Offering the populace
a vehicle for unity, baseball soon crossed social and racial barriers.

Colonial Cubans were not only seeking political independence from Spain, they yearned to establish a distinct culture.
Baseball helped define this new culture, a culture uniquely Cuban.
Its very acceptance was a rejection of the Spaniards' favored pastime, bullfighting. The demonization of bullfighting, and the
glorification of baseball, provided a means for Cubans to refute
the old in favor of the new, shifting their cultural focus from Iberia
to the United States.[5]

In Cuba, encounters with Americans on baseball diamonds
began in 1868 when the Havana Baseball Club played a team from
an American schooner anchored at Matanzas. Matanzas is one of
the easternmost sugar cane farming areas of the country, sepa-
rated from the industry's center in western Cuba by the city of
Havana. The factories in Matanzas were more advanced than their
western competitors due to the purchase of modern machinery
from the United States, which, at first, required American crews
to operate and maintain it.[6] During their free time, these Americans engaged in baseball in and around Matanzas, playing with
locals who were already passionate about the game. Perhaps this
influence explains why Matanzas eventually produced many of
Cuba's greatest players.[7]

In 1878, the first professional baseball team from the United States visited Cuba. It was the Hop Bitters nine, a team sponsored by a patent medicine company. In what was called "barnstorming," baseball teams took extended trips playing games with an eye toward profitability. Barnstorming had begun in the United States in the late 1860s but the Hop Bitters team was the first to open Cuba's lucrative doors to the practice.

The United States military was another major conduit for the American influence on Cuban baseball. Just prior to the sinking of the U.S.S. *Maine* in Havana harbor in 1898, the act that precipitated the U.S. entrance into the Spanish-American War, a baseball team from the ship defeated a Cuban team in a game near the harbor. The explosion on the *Maine* killed all but one of the U.S. players.[8] At the end of the Spanish-American War, a provisional force from the United States occupied the island for four years. Teams from the two countries played many games against one another.

In December of 1878, the Havana Baseball Club, the Matanzas Baseball Club, and the Almendares Baseball Club organized Cuba's first championship. Each team would play a series of three games against the other two. The prize was, true to baseball tradition, a pennant, a white silken flag paid for by the losers. The teams played on Sundays or holidays, using the rules published in the 1878 Spalding Baseball Guide.[9] Habana BBC took the pennant in that inaugural 1878-79 season, winning all of their games but one.

As professionalism crept into Cuban baseball in the 1870s, many of the upper-class players quit the original teams, opposed, in accord with the Edwardian mores of the era, to professionalism in sport. The trend toward pay proved inexorable, however, and Cuban baseball headed toward meritocracy, with skill surpassing class status as the requisite for the players.

With this shift, the color barrier in Cuban baseball began to break down. The trend toward professionalism was completed in the years after the War of Independence in 1898 and brought Afro-Cuban stars to the fore. But players of European descent continued to dominate the rosters and there was widespread resistance to the racial integration of the league.

The Liga Nacional de Baseball dissolved in 1900 due to opposition to the inclusion of two racially mixed teams, San Francisco and Cubano.[10] In the old league's place, the Liga Cubana was started. It was made up of four racially mixed teams: Cubano, San Francisco, Habana, and Almendarista.

Armando Marsans was born in Matanzas, Cuba, about 55 miles east of Havana, on October 3, 1885. Marsans's early life was one of privilege. His father was a first generation Cuban and a successful merchant. His mother was Cuban of Spanish descent. Armando Marsans's youth is nearly entirely unknown. Various reports state that the Marsans family fled colonial Cuba's unrest prior to the Spanish-American War, when Marsans was about ten years old. This puts the date of their alleged departure around 1895. One report, repeated several times in the press during Marsans's baseball career in the United States, claimed that the Marsans family was forced to leave Cuba because Armando had been caught by the Spanish authorities trading cigarettes for ammunition, which he would give to members of the Cuban insurgency. Whether this account is true or not, Armando Marsans and his family reportedly left Cuba for New York, where they remained for at least one year, and probably more. The story continues that Armando Marsans learned to play baseball in New York's Central Park during his family's exile, but in all likelihood, Marsans had been exposed to baseball prior to his family's reported exile.

By the time Marsans joined the Cincinnati Reds, and perhaps as early as their return to the United States, Marsans and his family had relocated in Havana. Marsans was one of at least four brothers, and he and his siblings, Raúl, Mario, and younger brother Francisco lived Havana at 78 Crespo Street.

Though Marsans's baseball talents and love of the game kept him in a nearly year-round baseball schedule, he was a young man of many interests and pursuits. Armando was a newsboy for the *Havana Post* and would eventually write for the paper. By 1914, Marsans and his father would be co-owners of a large tobacco factory producing cigars under the Fabrica de Tobacos de A. Marsans y Ca. label.

In Havana, on April 3, 1905, the Almendares Baseball Club beat the Habana Baseball Club five to four in front of more than eight thousand fans to clinch the league title. Playing left field for Almendares and batting in the ignominious eighth slot was an eighteen-year-old boy with a face still fat with youth. He was Armando Marsans, and he distinguished himself that day with two hits in three at bats.

Abel Linares, the mustachioed manager of the Almendares team, who wore pince-nez glasses on his prominent nose, had taken a Cuban team on a barnstorming tour of the United States each summer since 1902. Though the 1905 team was composed primarily of players from the Almen-dares nine, it was called the All Cubans. They billed themselves as the champions of Cuba and planned to display the silver Spalding Cup they had earned as victors of La Liga Habanera de Base-Ball as proof of their claim.

With a full schedule of games, and the grandiose plan of challenging the American and National League pennant winners to determine the true world's champion, Abel Linares

Armando Marsans around 1914. Jacinto Calvo, another early Cuban player in the U.S., named Marsans as the most intelligent of all the Cubans to play in the U.S. in the teens and twenties. (National Baseball Hall of Fame Library, Cooperstown, N.Y.)

and his baseball team boarded the S.S. *Monterrey* on May 16. Devoted fans of the Almendares Club rented a tugboat that day and, with a band playing on board, escorted the *Monterrey* out of Havana harbor. The players lined up on deck: Luis Bustamente, the shortstop from the Fe club, known as "Anguilla" or "eel," would become a star in the American Negro Leagues; From the Havana Baseball Club came the light-skinned Rogelio Valdes and his Afro-Cuban teammate, José Muñoz; The Almendares club supplied A. D'Meza and Agustín "Tinti" Molina, the white catcher and future Cuban baseball impresario, as well as Alfredo Cabrera, voted by his countrymen as the best baseball player in Cuba in 1903, and

Rafael Almeida and Armando Marsans.[11] Three other Almendares players were with them: Heliodoro "Jabuco" Hidalgo (his nickname meant "satchel" and referred to the dark-skinned outfielder's reliability with his glove), Emilio Palomino, and Almendares pitcher Inocencio Perez.[12] These were most of the top stars of Cuban baseball. Eight members of the racially mixed team later would be inducted into the Cuban Baseball Hall of Fame.

The All-Cubans played their first game in the United States on May 21, 1905, in Stamford, Connecticut. The All-Cubans triumphed five to three against a local nine at Keeler's Hill Field in front of an estimated three thousand fans, the largest crowd ever at the small field. Many of the overflow crowd sat on the grass, surrounding the playing field in a human ring several rows deep. The next day, the game was front-page news in the *Stamford Daily Advocate*, which reported, "The Cubans are, for the most part, undersized. Some of them are very boyish in appearance. They are remarkably active, and their fast fielding pleased the fans. They were fast, too, on the bases, and took all kinds of chances. Some of them kept up an incessant chatter in a language that sounded like a dialect of Spanish."[13] Rafael Almeida, playing third base for "the dusky men from the Island Republic," made an especially strong impression, being called "about as good a baseball player as ever chucked a ball across the diamond here."[14]

From this auspicious beginning, the All-Cubans traveled the East Coast from Massachusetts to Virginia, playing local and semipro teams, and drawing large crowds of curious baseball fans who came to see how Cubans had adopted their national game. The team returned to Cuba on September 19, having won seventy-eight of the one hundred games they played.[15]

2

Foreigners in a Foreign Land

The uniformed teams from New Britain and Hartford, Connecticut, jumped off the squat wooden streetcars followed by the band, instruments in hand, and entered Electric Field. The teams paraded around the diamond to the loud applause of the fans. After the teams warmed up, the Mayor of New Britain made his obligatory opening day speech. He then walked to the mound, pulled his hat down on his head, and threw an impressive ceremonial first pitch. The Mayor jogged back to the stands to a generous ovation and the 1908 New Britain Mountaineers took the field. Armando Marsans ran out to his position in left field, having reached the end of an eighteen-month odyssey to play for a team in the United States.

In November of 1906, a team called the All-Americans, managed by H.D. Ramsey, arrived in Cuba for a series of games against Havana's baseball teams. In the games against the Cuban teams, Ramsey's American nine dominated the Havana Reds but could not beat Marsans's Almendares team. Marsans played well in the games and impressed Ramsey. At Ramsey's invitation, Marsans played for the All-Americans in their final games in Cuba. Ramsey

11

convinced Marsans, and his teammate Alfredo Cabrera, to sign a contract to play with him in the United States in the 1907 season. "These two men are the stars of the Almendares team, the Cuban champions, and there is little doubt that they will make good in fast company in the States."[1]

Cabrera, known as "Pájaro" (Bird), was a gifted middle infielder who coupled a competent bat with exceptional defensive skills. He was born in the Canary Islands, a member of the islands' indigenous people. One American newspaper would describe Cabrera as "a slim, reddish brown man, with a face that bears the stamp of weariness of the ages—the face of a patient member of a conquered people."[2]

Marsans and Cabrera signed Ramsey's contracts on December 26, 1906. The Cubans would each receive $125 per month beginning May 1st. The All-Americans left Havana on New Year's Day, 1907, with Ramsey agreeing to notify Marsans and Cabrera, upon his return to the United States, where the two would play that summer.

Soon after Ramsey left Havana, Marsans and Cabrera heard he was going to manage a team in the new Atlantic League. The Atlantic League was not a part of the National Agreement, the overarching accord that bound most professional baseball leagues in the United States together. If Marsans and Cabrera were to play in this "outlaw" league, they would risk being blacklisted by organized baseball, preventing the Cubans from playing in any league that was a part of the National Agreement.

Fearing this outcome, Marsans and Cabrera signed contracts for the 1907 season with the Holyoke, Massachusetts, team of the Connecticut League. On February 1, however, Ramsey notified them he was the new manager of the Scranton, Pennsylvania, team in the New York State League, which was a part of organized baseball. Ramsey told Marsans and Cabrera to report to Scranton for the 1907 season.

The Cubans claimed that because Ramsey was not the manager of the Scranton team when they signed with him, their contracts were not valid.[3] The Holyoke management took the case to the National Association of Baseball Clubs, which ruled in favor of Scranton. Holyoke then asked the Connecticut League Secretary to take the case to the National Board of Arbitration. Again, the ruling was against Holyoke. Holyoke's last chance was a ruling from the National Commission, a three-man board charged with resolving all disputes arising in leagues that had signed the National Agreement.

The National Commission refused to free the Cubans from their obligation to Scranton.[4] After the National Commission ruled on June 5th, the Cubans chose to return to Cuba instead of report to Scranton. Scranton did not reserve either player after the 1907 season, meaning they were again free to sign with any team.

For several days in late April, while the case was pending before the National Commission, Marsans and Cabrera had visited Holyoke. The Holyoke players did not warmly receive the two Cubans, due to their belief that Marsans and Cabrera were of African descent. The *Holyoke Daily Transcript* said, "Some fans have an idea that the Cubans are negroes or may have negro blood. Such is not the case and a visit to the ball field will not contaminate."[5] The question of ethnicity voiced in this statement would persistently follow Marsans during his time in the United States.

In the spring of 1908, a *Havana Post* reporter recommended Marsans and Cabrera to manager Charles Humphrey of the New Britain, Connecticut team. Humphrey attempted to sign the Cubans throughout the spring and, finally, he received Marsans and Cabrera's signed contracts in mid–April.[6] Two other Cubans subsequently signed with New Britain: Luis Padron and Rafael Almeida.

The Cubans encountered problems even before they arrived in New Britain. The Connecticut League considered barring the players from the league based on the accusation they were of African descent.[7] The controversy was quelled by the local newspapers, which assured "They are all white men"[8] and also printed, "These men are strictly white and must not be confounded with the colored players known as the Cuban Giants. If it were not so they would not be allowed to play in the league and the manager has been very careful to inquire into this before signing them. They are really Spaniards in sense of blood descent."[9]

Of the three other Cubans who had signed with New Britain for the 1908 season, only Luis Padron was with Marsans on opening day. Padron had played baseball in the United States for two seasons prior to 1908—with Poughkeepsie in the Hudson River League in 1906 and Brooklyn, of the Atlantic League, in 1907.[10] Padron was a prodigious baseball talent at the plate, in the field, and on the mound. He had a long face but there were no hard angles to it. His jaw line, his nose, and his lips were all rounded. It was these last two features, his broad nose and his full lips, in combination with his skin tone and dark hair that led to accusations, which may have been true, that Padron had African ancestry. The stereotypical image of people of African descent was well-seated in the mind of the American public. Padron's appearance was close enough to this image to trigger the suspicion that he was of African descent. The assumption was made easier by the Americans' perception that most Cubans had at least some African heritage.

Marsans and Padron had arrived in New Britain on April 22nd with the first threat to their eligibility based on ethnicity averted.

Havana Dicember 20th 1912   "1080" Box 194

Mr August Herrman

    Cincinati

      Ohio.

      Dear Sir-

        I beg to inform you that I have been appointed Manager of the Havana Club of this City and take this opportunity to ask you have any objections in me doing so. I have consulted the Doc respecting my physical condition so as to be in good training when I return to the Club by next season, and he advises me not to be idle, but me some excersise so as to have my limbs in good shape. Therefore I play only twice a week.

I will further state that I am practising to Catch in which position I am making quite a success and hope to fill this position if needed at an time for the Cincinati.

And hoping you'll be in a good health I remain very respectfully yours

As this signature apparently confirms, the full name of the man known to baseball history as Rafael Almeida was probably Rafael D'Almeida.

They checked in at the Hotel Beloin on unpaved Church Street, where most of the players stayed for the season.[11] The two Cubans had four days to practice with their new team before the opening game. Marsans showed well in the outfield and also impressed on the basepaths.[12] He won a starting position in the outfield, but Padron was confined to his room in the Beloin Hotel due to illness. He soon recovered and began practicing with his new team. Local children were permitted to watch Marsans, Padron, and the rest of the team practice until players began to complain that their gloves and balls were disappearing. They were undoubtedly put to good use in the local sandlot games.[13]

From the beginning, Marsans and Padron made good impressions with their play and provoked Manager Humphrey to think about "sending a special steamer down to the island to pick up a few insurgents, who now that there are no more insurrections to be stirred up are willing to play ball for a living."[14]

On June 10th, Rafael Almeida became the third Cuban to join the New Britain Mountaineers. He had toured the U.S. three years before with Marsans and the All Cubans. Almeida was a light-skinned Cuban from an exceptionally wealthy family of Portuguese extraction and was a fop of the first order, always elegantly dressed. He was twenty years old at the beginning of the 1908 season. Almeida had a narrow, long face, and a prominent, patrician nose. His skin tone and facial features, together with his extreme wealth, cleared a path for Almeida free from indictment about mixed ethnic heritage.

Almeida's ethnic heritage seemed to be free of African influence, but the protests about ethnicity the Cubans would face cannot be entirely refuted. Though it can be said that Padron was probably of partial African descent, this possibility cannot be definitively ruled out for Marsans, Cabrera, or even the light skinned Almeida. There is no evidence that this was the case for any of these three men, but such a fact, had it been true, would most likely have been a closely guarded family secret in race-conscious Cuba. In the segregated world of baseball in 1908, the doors to white baseball were strictly guarded and even the hint of controversy about a player having African heritage could have prevented him from stepping on the field. But American baseball had not always been that way.

Bud Fowler was the first African-American to play baseball professionally when he joined an all-white team in Pennsylvania in

1872.[15] Fowler was a talented and versatile player who excelled as a second baseman. As the first of more than sixty African-American men to play in white leagues before 1900, Fowler soon was joined by Moses Fleetwood Walker. The son of a physician, Walker attended Oberlin College and the University of Michigan. After earning varsity letters in 1882 and '83 at Michigan, Walker became a professional player with the Toledo club of the Northwestern League. Toledo entered the American Association the following year with Walker as its catcher, making him the first African-American to play in the major leagues, sixty-two years before Jackie Robinson.

The year 1886 found four African-Americans in white baseball: Walker, Fowler, Frank Grant, and George Stovey. Frank Grant was born in Massachusetts and began playing professionally with the Meriden, Connecticut, team in the Eastern League. When the team disbanded in mid-season, Grant and two teammates went to play in Buffalo. It was reported in the local paper that Grant was a Spaniard, apparently to deflect any bigotry.[16]

The confusion that many Americans held about ethnicity is evident in this story. Americans' unfamiliarity with Hispanics, and therefore, their inability to distinguish them from African-Americans allowed Grant to pass as being of Spanish Descent.

The National Association of Baseball Players had been the first to establish a color barrier in baseball in 1867 when they voted to restrict any African-American player, or any team with one or more African-American players on its roster, from membership. Professionalism soon brought an end to the Association comprised of amateurs, and the steadily growing number of African-American professional players provoked predictions of a future of completely integrated baseball. But antipathy toward the African-Americans slowly grew.

On July 14, 1887, racial tension surfaced at a mid-summer meeting of the International League. The league allowed its five African-Americans to continue playing. But, fearing the defection of its best, and bigoted, white players, the league specified no more African-Americans could be signed to play in the league. The prohibition met protest from newspapers in northern cities, with the *Newark Call* printing the following:

> If anywhere in the world the social barriers are broken down it is on the ball field. There, many men of low birth and poor breeding are the idols of the rich and cultured; the best man is

he who plays best. Even men of churlish disposition and coarse hues are tolerated on the field. In view of these facts the objection to colored men is ridiculous. If social distinctions are to be made, half the players in the country will be shut out. Better make character and personal habits the test. Weed out the toughs and intemperate men first, and then it may be in order to draw the color line.[17]

July 14, 1887, was an infamous day in the relationship between professional baseball and African-Americans. On the same day the International League wrote the prohibition against the signing of African-American players, Adrian "Cap" Anson, the greatest baseball star of his day, refused to field his team in an exhibition game with the Newark Little Giants because George Stovey, the Little Giants' African-American pitcher, was scheduled to play. Stovey did not play, claiming he was sick, and the confrontation was averted.

Anson had shown his prejudice before. In 1883, his Chicago White Stockings were scheduled to play an exhibition against the Toledo team with "Fleet" Walker on its roster. Anson threatened to cancel the game if Walker played. The manager of the Toledo team told Anson that if Walker were not allowed to play, the game would not be held. Anson was not only a bigot but, apparently, more committed to money than to his beliefs. When faced with the possibilities of losing his team's share of the gate receipts, Anson chose to play the game with Walker on the field.[18]

Many of the players of the day, as well as baseball executives, shared Anson's views. In September of 1887, eight members of the St. Louis Browns refused to play an exhibition against the Cuban Giants, an African-American team, and the St. Louis owner was forced to tell seven thousand fans, who had already paid admission, that his team had fallen ill and the game was cancelled.

Some African-Americans saw that segregation in baseball was imminent and chose to form all black teams. The most dominant African-American team of the last years of the nineteenth century was the Cuban Giants. The headwaiter at a summer resort for affluent New Yorkers on Long Island's southern shore formed the team. The team comprised waiters at the hotel and entertained the guests playing nine games that first summer of 1885. After the hotel closed for the season, the team took to the road on a barnstorming trip. The "Cuban" in their name came from the fact that they attempted to pass as Cubans to add an exotic flavor to their team, sometimes speaking a jibberish they hoped would pass for Spanish on the field.[19]

Baseball had seized the hearts of African-Americans as strongly as those of other groups of American culture. By the late 1880s African-American teams had sprung up throughout the East. But as segregation solidified, fewer African-Americans played in white leagues. The years 1892–1895 saw no African-Americans playing on the white side of segregated baseball, and the last African-American team to play in a white league was the Acme Colored Giants in the Iron and Oil League in 1898.

Competition between African-Americans and whites on professional baseball diamonds, however, did not end. Teams from each side of segregated baseball continued to face one another in exhibition games. The 1908 New Britain Mountaineers had played one such exhibition earlier that spring, before Marsans joined the team, against the African-American Philadelphia Giants team.

The first year for the New Britain Mountaineers franchise in the Connecticut League was 1908. Electric Field had been upgraded through spring training to accommodate the new team. The players had watched the completion of the additions to the grandstand, and the small fences in front of it built to prevent the crowd from interfering with the game, during their twice-a-day practices.[20] Two new entrances to the park had also been constructed, one for spectators on foot and another for carriages and automobiles that would park near left field. Electric Field's outfield was so small that, mid-way through the season, flags were placed on the outfield fences at points in right and left field. It was declared that any ball clearing the fences to the foul-territory side of the flags would not receive a home run but only a double. Balls clearing the fence to the centerfield side of the flags would still be scored as home runs.[21]

Marsans continued to distinguish himself in the small outfield and also offensively. His batting average placed him in the top ten in the league in the middle of the season, but it was not just Marsans's batting that made an impression. His intelligent style of play was also acknowledged: "Marsans, the Cuban, tried a slick trick yesterday, but it didn't go through. With a Springfield man on second, the Cuban hustled to the base from leftfield, catching the runner napping, but there was no ball at the base, so the trick was lost. It shows Marsans is crafty. He did some stunning outfield work for New Britain yesterday."[22]

Marsans even garnered kudos in *Sporting Life*, one of the

nationally distributed periodicals primarily dedicated to baseball. *Sporting Life* reported, "Marsans, the Cuban player, who is covering left for New Britain, is hitting finely and fielding fast. He is a swift runner, and on the bases must be watched all the time."[23] The outstanding performance of Marsans and his Cuban teammates was enough to turn things around for the weak New Britain club, and they began to climb in the Connecticut League standings.[24]

Luis Padron, after a slow start, had emerged as one of the best players on the New Britain team. Padron was a talented, if sometimes erratic, pitcher. He was also an exceptional hitter who battled for the league batting title. Padron and Marsans's performance won them popularity with the New Britain fans but continuing controversy about the Cubans' ethnicity threatened to overshadow their successes on the diamond. The protests began to focus on Padron. He was called "the near–Cuban,"[25] "the browned-up boy,"[26] and "dusky Padron" with his "watermelon grin"[27] and opposing fans threw things at him while he stood on the mound.[28]

In mid–June, the Mountaineers took a road trip without Luis Padron. "Pitcher Padron, who claims to be Cuban, was left at home, as the visiting management figured that a hostile crowd would soon discover his secret. The two real Cubans, Marsans and Almeida, were headliners and each distinguished himself by fine play."[29] There are two possible interpretations of this statement. Either the author is accusing Padron of being an African-American posing as a Latino to be eligible to play or the author is espousing the popular view of the time that the only people who could be truly called Cubans were those without African heritage. Almeida was exempt from these accusations because of his light skin and fine features, and probably also because of his exceptional wealth. Marsans's, on the other hand, was not always beyond question. His olive skin, wide nose, full lips, and black hair supplied bigots with enough ammunition to harass him.

Alfredo Cabrera had been the most reticent of the four Cubans that signed New Britain contracts. In communications through the spring Cabrera never stated when he would come to New Britain. New Britain's new owner, William Hanna, had continued to lure the Cuban shortstop to New Britain. Cabrera finally joined his three countrymen at the beginning of July. After Cabrera's first game it seemed Hanna's efforts had been worthwhile, Cabrera "played a smashing game at short and pulled off one stop

that earned his salary right there. He has a smooth-working wing
[throwing arm] and at the bat he was not a bit timid."[30]

On July 7th, Luis Padron stepped to the plate with Cabrera
on first base in the bottom of the ninth inning and hit a pinch-hit
home run. The vast majority of New Britain fans never voiced bias
against Padron based on his questioned ethnicity, and the question seemed to be entirely forgotten in the celebration. "The
bleachers emptied before he got half way around the field and the
fans spread over the field and brought him home like a triumphant
Roman general."[31] Manager William Hanna, who had recently purchased the team, presented his "dark-hued workman" with a ten-
dollar bill on the field as a bonus.[32]

On July 17, the owner of the Hartford team filed an official
protest against the Cuban players with the secretary of the league,
claiming the Cubans were ineligible due to African heritage.[33] The
owners subsequently reached an agreement in which they vowed
to no longer officially challenge the Cubans's eligibility if New
Britain did not play Padron on road trips.

But in the second game of a double-header in Springfield
soon after the meeting, Manager Hanna decided to pitch Padron.
Padron walked out to the mound to applause from the small contingent of New Britain supporters. Dan O'Neil, the Springfield
manager, was outraged. O'Neil pulled out a roll of money and
offered to bet Hanna one hundred dollars to five dollars that
O'Neil would succeed in having Padron banned from the league
at the owners' meeting that night.

O'Neil spoke to several New Britain players, urging them to
take a stand against playing on the same team as the Cubans
because of their alleged African descent. None of the New Britain
players complied.[34] At the owners' meeting that night, O'Neil was
not able to convince enough team owners and League officials
that the Cubans should be banned from the league. He took his
revenge the next time his team played New Britain. With Padron
on the mound, O'Neil instructed his coaches at first and third
base to taunt Padron with racial epithets.[35]

It seemed obvious to one reporter that it was not just opposing
fans and management that had turned against the Cubans. The
New Britain Herald published a lengthy article decrying alleged
injustices dealt to the Cubans by league umpires:

> Every fair-minded patron of baseball in this league and certainly

every baseball reporter and scorer is aware that certain of the umpires—the majority of them in fact—are not giving some of the players on the New Britain team a fair show at the bat. We refer to the Cubans, whose standing in this league, legally backed as they are by the credentials of the national commission, is even with that of the other players, born in this country, England, Ireland or Germany.

During the week closed, the balls which Umpires Wilkinson and Kennedy called as strikes on Marsans, Almeida, Cabrera, and Padron were disgraceful. So outrageous were their classification as strikes that it is impossible to accredit it to an error of the arbiter of the plate.

It is charged that the umpires, aided and abetted, secretly, by some of the misguided owners and managers, are following a well-laid plot to deprive the Cubans of their superior batting averages....

The scheme is to force these Cuban players—by long odds the most gentlemanly players on the diamond to-day—out of the league.

Shame on the managers who countenance these tactics. There are no words too contemptuous to apply to the umpires who are their willing tools.

It is the earnest hope that the managers who have stooped to this scheme will bring down the wrath of the fans, who desire to see clean, fair ball, upon their heads. Empty box offices will be the result should these methods of retaliating against the Cubans be continued, while hair-brained owners in blatant language declare to the audiences that they will drive the Cubans out of the league.[36]

Despite the alleged impartiality of league umpires, Marsans and the other Cubans continued their great play. One local writer believed Marsans and two other players on the team "were looked upon as probable candidates for some of the major league clubs."[37] By late August, Padron, undeterred by the controversy about his ethnicity, was battling for the league batting crown. He would finish just one point behind the league leader with a .313 batting average, especially impressive considering the highest team batting average in the league was an anemic .235.[38]

Luis Padron did not return to the New Britain team for the 1909 season. Hanna's stated reason for not offering him another contract was his unpopularity with the other players "owing to his 'big-headedness.'"[39] In the history of baseball, "big-headedness" has seldom prevented the signing of exceptionally talented players.

The more plausible explanation is the specter of continued controversy regarding Padron's ethnicity.

With Padron gone, Marsans and Cabrera became the focus of the protests. Prior to the 1909 season, the league again considered banning them from play "on the ground that they are really negroes," according to *Sporting Life*.[10] Almeida was again exempt from this sort of accusation.

William Hanna responded to the article with the following letter, printed in the March 13th *Sporting Life*:

> I read to-day in this week's Sporting Life, under the head of Telegraph Notes, something that greatly surprised me, viz., that my Cuban players were to be expelled by the Connecticut League, as they were not Cubans, but negroes. This is false in every particular. The Connecticut League has never taken this matter up. Their color is well-known to every manager in this league, as I hold certificates of birth from each and every one of them, countersigned by the American consul in Cuba, and they are all Spaniards. Furthermore, they are gentlemen and good ball players. I think you have done them an injustice, and it might be the means of causing them to stay away, which you could understand would be a great loss to me...I trust you will make the correction in your next issue and if you have any doubt as to my statement I can furnish you proof on request.[11]

The season began without any Cubans on the team and it seemed as if Hanna's concerns about the Cubans not reporting were true but he received a letter from a friend of Cabrera's that read:

> My friend Alfredo Cabrera has asked me to write in his name as well as Marsans's and Almeida's explaining that it is impossible to leave before the 24th, as they play their last game the 22nd, and have a very good chance of winning the pennant, and the money that goes with it. They would like very much to be there already, but they think of the glory and money they would lose if they go now. So he tells me that they will surely leave Havana April 24, unless the impossible happens, which they hope will not happen.[12]

Cabrera, Almeida, and Marsans did sail from Havana on the evening of Saturday, April 24th, having won the Liga General de Base Ball de La Republica de Cuba championship that afternoon. The New Britain Herald took the opportunity to poke fun at

Almeida. "Senor Al has taken passage on the most palatial steamer on the line out of Havana and has chartered a freighter that will plough the waves in the wake of the passenger boat. The second boat is at present being loaded with Al's suits, headgear, and neckwear. A large section of the hold has been set apart for his shoes and fancy hosiery."[43]

Marsans, Cabrera, and Almeida were expected to arrive in New York and to come directly to New Britain on April 27th.[44] Instead, the trio spent Tuesday night in New York, without reporting to New Britain as scheduled. The next day, they met the New Britain team in Bridgeport, watched the game there, and then went to New Britain and checked into the Hotel Beloin.[45]

When they again donned the dark blue uniforms of New Britain, Marsans, Almeida, and Cabrera were greeted warmly by the fans—"They play the game so heartily and so well that they are popular with the crowd, and were very heartily welcomed back by them."[46] Arriving in great physical condition from the recent Cuban baseball season, Marsans was soon racing around the outfield making spectacular plays. His play in the 11–5 win against Waterbury on May 2nd was described this way, "The game was featured by a barehanded catch by outfielder Marsans in the 8th, with runners on first and second, Sillery hit a fly close to the line in left field. Marsans had to make a great sprint to get near the ball ... the catch was one of the finest ever seen ... and gained the Cuban much applause."[47]

Within two weeks of their arrival, Cabrera led the New Britain team in batting with a .318 average. Marsans was second on the team with eight hits in seven games, including a home run, for a .276 average. Almeida was batting .250 with four stolen bases in nine games.[48] Their performance helped the New Britain team make a great stride toward the top of the league.

The formal protests about the Cubans' ethnicity had come to an end. Whether or not another agreement had been reached among the owners is not known, but the Cubans were not only free from the threat of being banned from play but there were no more complaints about biased umpiring for the rest of their time in New Britain.

On May 9th, Rafael Almeida became ill with what was described as a hard cold, tonsillitis, or "Yankee grip" depending on the source.[49] The illness kept Almeida out of several games and landed him in the New Britain hospital.[50] Marsans, suffering from bronchitis, joined Almeida as a patient.[51] Both men recovered quickly and rejoined the team.

But Armando Marsans soon checked back into the clapboard Victorian house that had been converted into the New Britain General Hospital. His case of bronchitis had re-emerged after only one game in Bridgeport. The dying patient in the bed next to Marsans unsettled the Cuban. The man received a constant stream of visitors, who disappeared behind the screen separating the patient from Marsans, but Marsans could hear sobbing and expressions of grief.[52] One article claimed the manager of the rival Hartford team intentionally placed Marsans next to the dying man to scare the Cuban.[53] If true, the plan apparently worked, for, though he was improving, Marsans believed he was very sick and might be in mortal danger. He requested permission from team owner William Hanna to go home to Cuba.[54] Hanna brought Almeida and Cabrera to the hospital to visit Marsans. They tried to convince him that he was not as ill as he thought and that he should remain in New Britain.[55] Their mission was unsuccessful. Marsans left for Cuba on the 18th of May. Marsans was still just twenty years old and homesickness, perhaps aggravated by his illness, is the most plausible explanation for his return home.

While Marsans was in Cuba, the team's promising performance flagged forcing Hanna to ask retired National League umpire Thomas Lynch, a New Britain resident, to manage the team. Lynch agreed to a three-week test period after which he would make a final decision. Lynch knew the game of baseball but had difficulty commanding the respect of the New Britain players. After having his orders ignored several times on the field, the square-jawed, mustachioed, new manager decided to buy a portion of the team from Hanna to give him more authority with the players. This move would have a significant effect upon the careers of Almeida and Marsans when Lynch was later named President of the National League.

Late July brought two significant developments regarding the New Britain team. Luis Padron's name resurfaced. The Cuban referred to as the "same colored chap who played with New Britain last season" was given a try out with the Chicago White Sox.[56] Padron was ridiculed openly about his heritage by the big leaguers and did not make the team. Though Padron was unsuccessful, his tryout speaks to the rising awareness in organized baseball about the talents of Cuban players.

The second development concerned Armando Marsans's return to New Britain. Marsans wrote Almeida as early as the end of May saying he was recovering and was planning to return to New Britain.[57] When Marsans's desire to return from Cuba was made public in late July, the fans' excitement convinced the team owner to take the player back.[58] Marsans cabled his travel itinerary to manager Billy Hanna, saying he would arrive in New York on the 27th or 28th of July,[59] then notified the New Britain club he would report in early August.[60] But Marsans changed his mind, writing Hanna that he was still sick and would not report to New Britain at all.[61] It is difficult to believe that Marsans was still sick after two and a half months, and his failure to return was probably a manifestation of his desire to remain at home in Havana.

In Marsans's absence, Cabrera was impressing writers and fans. Cabrera compiled strong statistics for the 1909 season, leading the New Britain team with twenty-six stolen bases in 115 games and finishing with a .288 average. Despite a mid-season slump, Rafael Almeida batted .298 with twenty-nine doubles, seven triples, ten home runs and twenty-one stolen bases in 108 games.[62] The New Britain nine finished the season in third place with a 65–55 record, and did not go unnoticed by the major league teams. The Cincinnati Reds purchased "Swat" McCabe, the Cubans' New Britain teammate, in August.[63] These scouts must have also watched Cabrera and Almeida play and may have seen Marsans in action before his return to Cuba. Scouts from the Boston Braves of the National League were also following developments in New Britain, paying special attention to Almeida.[64]

In the spring of 1910, Marsans remained in Cuba cabling Hanna that he would not sail until the 15th of May.[65] Marsans explained his decision in a message he sent to New Britain with Cabrera that said he did not want to risk sickness due to unpleasant weather early in the season and thought a delay in his arrival was advisable.[66] Almeida also remained in Havana, announcing that he was holding out for more money, but Hanna declined to negotiate with him.[67]

New Britain's season did not begin well. The team's batting average of .198 was the worst in the league and they won only two of their first seventeen games. "Things became so bad in New Britain that the players could not go out on the streets at night for fear of being assaulted. For the past week they have been daily subjected to insult after insult."[68] At the end of April, the team's

listless play forced Hanna to settle with Almeida. He wired the
Cuban in Havana telling him to report to New Britain with the
understanding Almeida would get his requested raise.[69]

Attendance suffered as New Britain's lackluster season progressed. William Hanna decided to sell the team. He accepted an
offer of $3500 without negotiation, despite his asking price of
$4500. Thomas Lynch had become president of the National
League and had apparently sold his share of the team back to
Hanna. The transaction took place at a racetrack and took less
than five minutes. Dan O'Neil, the new owner, posted his son at
Electric Field's turnstiles and took his place on the New Britain
bench to begin managing his new team.[70]

Dan O'Neil was a career baseball man. He had served as a
scout for the Pittsburgh Pirates and had owned and managed the
Springfield team in the Connecticut League when the Cubans pre-
miered in 1908 and had vociferously protested their eligibility.

Gonzalo Sánchez, another Cuban, had joined Cabrera and
Marsans on the New Britain team in 1910 on Hanna's watch. Sánchez
was a wiry catcher who had played for Havana in the 1908–09 Cuban
season. As was the case with most Cuban players who came north
to play baseball, he was touted as "one of the best players ever developed" in Cuba.[71] O'Neil, however, released Sánchez at the end of
May. He had played as back up catcher, starting in several games,
but "the Cuban was handicapped by his lack of knowledge of English
as much as by his inability to come up to the standard."[72]

Under O'Neil's management the team turned around. O'Neil
sold a half interest of the team to Joe Connor.[73] Joe Connor, now the
Cubans' teammate and captain, "used to call them names that didn't
often get into print" when he had played against them as a member
of the Springfield team under O'Neil's management.[74] Now that the
Cubans were on his team, Connor, like O'Neil, made no protests. And
this was the case for most of Marsans's and the other Cubans' time
in New Britain. The vast majority of accusations against the Cubans
came from fans, players, and management of opposing teams. Their
bigotry was probably real, but their actions may have been intended
to rattle the Cubans or to have them declared ineligible to play, not
in the interest of maintaining the racial integrity of baseball, but to
gain an advantage in their games against New Britain.

But there were exceptions, and one of them occurred on July
22nd. It was the most curious event in Marsans's three and a half
seasons in New Britain. In the seventh inning of a game against

Bridgeport, Cabrera went to bat. On the bench, Marsans became embroiled in an argument that led to a fight with his own team's catcher. The entire team became involved in the wrangle, much to the amazement and delight of the Bridgeport crowd. The fight was broken up and the umpire ejected Marsans for fighting with one of his teammates.

That player was "Nig" Rufiage. "Nig" was short for "nigger," apparently because the man had wavy, short, black hair. Catchers take more physical abuse than any other players, crouching behind the plate, being hit by foul tips, and blocking wild pitches. Rufiage was up to the challenge. He was "an old campaigner and it takes more than an ordinary accident to put him out of commission. He caught yesterday with two of his fingers swollen twice their natural size and the nail was hanging off one of them."[75]

Even in the Connecticut League of 1910, being ejected for fighting with a teammate was an extraordinary occurrence. The limited coverage the event received in the papers leaves much to speculation. What is certain is that this was the only time Marsans was ejected during his tenure in New Britain. The most plausible explanation for the fight is that Rufiage, who, judging by his nickname, was the focus of racist taunting, turned that same cruelty on either Cabrera, at bat, or Marsans on the bench, incensing Marsans to a degree that provoked him to fight.[76]

This event marks an important moment in Marsans's personal development. Marsans, who the season before had lacked the maturity to remain or return to New Britain after his illness, was now acting in a confident manner. Though perhaps still lacking maturity, Marsans standing up to one of his toughest teammates because of what he perceived as an insult to his honor, or that of Cabrera's, hints that Marsans was gaining confidence as a person.

The Cuban was also developing confidence as a player. In one 19-game stretch, Marsans batted .432 with thirty-two hits. He raised his overall average from a low of .205 on June 20th, to above .300 for much of the second half of the season. The season ended with Marsans batting .292 in 102 games, the best batting average on the New Britain team, which, combined with forty-five stolen bases, made the young Cuban a bona fide star in the league and gained him notice from the major league teams.[77]

Another example of dissent from New Britain's generally unified support of the Cubans occurred at the beginning of the 1911 season. Luis Padron expressed a desire to play for New Britain

again after two seasons in the West, but was not signed.[78] One fan
wrote the following letter to the *New Britain Herald*:

> Sporting Editor New Britain Herald:—Will you kindly give
> this space in your valuable paper which will voice the senti-
> ments of hundreds of ball fans in New Britain?... "Why doesn't
> Dan O'Neil get Louis Padron?" He certainly has won a warm
> spot in the hearts of all fair-minded sports by his conduct and
> consistent work on the bases and with the stick. Now if there
> are one or two players on the team that don't want to play with
> him it is up to the management to see that they do and to this
> end there is now being circulated a petition in several shops
> asking Dan O'Neil to get Louis here and several hundred have
> signed willingly and more to come. Respectfully, A Fan[79]

The letter provoked a response from another fan: "Dear Sir—
In your issue of last evening we read of a suggestion signed 'A Fan'
in regard to Louis Padron. It is the same old story of someone trying to run another man's business. Louis Padron was really a good
asset at times, but at other times he was like a good many other
players with a thousand dollar arm and a ten cent head, more
likely the latter...."[80]

If Padron was unpopular with some of the New Britain fans,
there was no lack of affection for the remaining three Cubans on
the team. "The news that the Cubans are coming back was received
with joy by the fans in this city. There is probably no better liked
trio in the League than Almeida, Cabrera, and Marsans, and everyone is tickled that they're going to wear the New Britain uniform
once more."[81] Armando Marsans and Alfredo Cabrera both
reported on April 22nd, twelve days after the first practice. Cabrera started the 1911 season impressively, batting .328 in the first
eighteen games. Marsans, was hitting only .250, but had already
stolen eighteen bases.[82] Almeida, though still reserved by New
Britain, did not report to the club in 1911. He claimed the legal
difficulties surrounding his uncle's $300,000 estate demanded his
constant presence in Havana.[83] By mid–May, the fans' fondness for
Almeida, "the recalcitrant child,"[84] began to fade.

In 1911, Marsans again dominated opponents on the base
paths and was declared by the *New Britain Herald* to be "so far
ahead of all other base stealers that there isn't any comparison."[85]
After a 2–0 victory against Hartford he was heralded in the papers.

"Marsans was the hero of the game. He scored the first run on a clean steal of home, just missed stealing home in the first inning, and saved the game for New Britain in the eighth by a sensational one-hand catch. He was hailed as the conquering hero by the adoring New Britain crowd, and when he came in from the outfield after his wonderful feat he was met by the mascot and presented with one of O'Neil's crisp, new five dollar bills."[86] Marsans's play earned him kudos as the "best all-around man on the team."[87] In this one game Marsans demonstrated how far he had advanced as a baseball player in his time in New Britain. Stealing home base is one of the most brazen things a player can do on the diamond. That Marsans was willing to try it a second time, after being tagged out in an attempt in the first inning, illustrates that Marsans was playing with a high level of confidence in his abilities.

Though Marsans had developed significantly as a player and had begun to mature as a person, he was still a young man. After a game on May 16 Marsans left a note in his locker. The note read "Dan O'Neil, Dear Sir: Would write a few words to tell you that my mother is sick and I got to go home. I will be back as soon as I can. Armando Marsans."[88] Marsans took the morning train to New York, saying nothing to the other players.

The reason Marsans left may have been the harsh criticism O'Neil gave him after being thrown out stealing second base without the manager's signal.[89] "Marsans offers one excuse for his disappearance—the sickness of his mother. But no one takes any stock in that and all believe that Marse has got 'cold feet' and is hiking for a warmer climate. He went so quickly and so suddenly that no one saw him going and there was great surprise in the ranks of the ball tossers this morning when Captain Waterman announced the dusky son of Cuba had gone, leaving his baseball clothes and other baseball effects but taking all his personal possessions with him."[90]

It is most probable that both events, his mother's illness and his argument with O'Neil, were true and that his emotional connection with his mother combined with the difficulty with his manager were enough to push the not-completely-mature Marsans home.

The first rumors of the sale of Marsans and Almeida to a major league team surfaced on June 15th about a month after Marsans's departure with a report that Cleveland had offered $1,000 for each of the Cubans.[91] Less than a week later it seemed Cincinnati would purchase Almeida and Marsans. On June 21st, the rumors gained credence when Dan O'Neil sailed to Cuba in search of Marsans and Almeida, motivated by Cincinnati's promise to pay $7500 for the Cubans if they made good in the major leagues.[92] But O'Neil had to deliver the Cubans in Cincinnati by July 1st. "The international game of hide and seek" came to an end when Marsans and Almeida appeared in New Britain on the 25th of June, having passed O'Neil at sea.[93]

Almeida and Marsans were expected to accompany the New Britain team to Springfield for its game on June 26th. "Marsans was right on the job and was tickled to go along. Almeida, however, turned up his nose at the proposition and said that he would not travel to Springfield with the New Britain team. Probably it is because the weather is too cold or somebody's feet are too cold or probably it is because someone has a swelled cranium because he has been sold to a big league club."[94] The two Cubans stayed in New Britain briefly and then, on June 28th, escorted by the club owner's son, they boarded a train headed for Cincinnati with a controversy awaiting them.[95] "The Reds have signed two players from the Connecticut League who have Spanish blood in their veins and are very dark skinned. As soon as the news spread that the Reds were negotiating for the Cubans a protest went up from the fans against introducing Cuban talent into the ranks of the major leagues," reported the *Cincinnati Tribune*.[96]

3

Opportunity

The train pulled into the Cincinnati station at seven o'clock on the evening of Wednesday, June 28th, 1911. Two young Cubans and their escort stepped down onto the platform amid the bustle of passengers and porters.

The palpable athleticism of their bodies was evident as the two young men walked along the platform, one with a bat in his hand. They were nattily dressed, according to the fashion of the time. Marsans wore a tan linen suit with a dark necktie, Almeida a dark suit and a wide floral pattern tie.

August Herrmann, the portly president and part owner of the Cincinnati Reds, was at the station to meet them. After brief salutations, he handed the agreed-upon sum to the Cubans' escort, who thanked Herrmann, and said goodbye. Herrmann was pleased by the politeness and humility of the Cubans, and relieved about their appearance. They were not, it was reported in the next day's paper, "small and swarthy in complexion," but showed, "practically no effects of the tropical heat and sun."[1]

Still, bringing foreign-born Latinos into the National League was going to be difficult. The United States was largely uninformed about Latin American culture at the beginning of the 20th century, and prejudice flourished.

The belief that white Americans were racially superior to Latinos was integral to the American view of the hemisphere. As Matthew Jacobson notes in *Barbarian Virtues*, this sentiment was evident as early as the 1850s, when the U.S. chargé d'affaires in Central America wrote, "If the United States, as compared with the Spanish American Republics, has achieved immeasurable advance in all elements, that result is eminently due to the rigid and inexorable refusal of the dominant Teutonic stock to debase its blood, impair its intellect, lower its moral standards, or peril its institutions by intermixture with the inferior and subordinate races of man. In obedience of heaven, it has rescued half a continent from savage beasts and still more savage men."[2]

The Mexican-American War of 1846–48 was one of the few times that the United States used military means to take permanent possession of land. Texas, which was already populated by American settlers, was a natural candidate to be integrated into the union, but what about Mexico itself? Jacobson writes (quoting from a contimporary source) that the thought of "the peons, Negroes, and Indians of all sorts, the wild tribe of the Commanches, the bug-and-lizard-eating 'Diggers,' and other half-monkey savages in those countries, as equal to the citizens of the United States" was disturbing enough to many to limit the annexation,[3] and in the end Mexico was allowed to retain its independence, though the United States appropriated much of what is now the Southwest from the its vanquished neighbor.

At the peak of worldwide imperialism, the United States generally eschewed overt colonization of foreign lands, instead choosing a path of intervention when countries strayed from the course the United States deemed acceptable. In *Barbarian Virtues*, President Roosevelt's corollary to the Monroe Doctrine presented in the 1904 annual message to Congress is cited as succinctly summarizing the position: "Chronic wrongdoing or an impotence which results in general loosening of civilized society, may in America, as elsewhere, ultimately require intervention by some civilized nation.... If every country washed by the Caribbean Sea would show progress in stable and just civilization which with the aid of the Platt Amendment, Cuba has shown ... all question of interference by this nation with their affairs would be at an end."[4]

The Platt Amendment to the Cuban Constitution was among

the boldest of U.S. interventions. After defeating Spain in the Spanish-American War, the United States took a paternalistic role with regard to the newly independent Cuba. The Amendment guaranteed the United States the right to intervene in Cuban affairs to preserve Cuban independence, to maintain a Cuban government adequate for the protection of its citizens' rights, and to claim land for naval or coaling stations. It also prohibited Cuba from making treaties with foreign powers on its own. In effect, Cuba was considered a vassal

August "Garry" Herrmann, who the *St. Louis Post Dispatch* (April 18, 1917) called the man "who put the wet in banquet," often traveled to away games in a private railcar loaded with lager, wine, sausage, and bread. (National Baseball Hall of Fame Library, Cooperstown, N.Y.)

state, its people incapable of working in their own best interest without the superior wisdom and strength of the United States to guide and protect them.

Cuba, with its strong Spanish heritage, cosmopolitan culture, and obliteration of indigenous peoples, was seen as a special case in comparison to the rest of Latin America. The people of countries like Mexico, where miscegenation had been widespread, were looked upon not so much as children, but as close to subhuman—a misbegotten race whose touch was to be feared, and a ghastly vision of what the U.S. itself might become if immigration was allowed to continue unchecked.

> What the Melting Pot actually does in practice can be seen in Mexico, where the absorption of the blood of the original Spanish conquerors by the native populations has produced the racial mixture we call Mexican and which is now engaged in demonstrating its incapacity for self-government....
>
> It must be born in mind that the specializations which characterize the higher races are of relatively recent development, are highly unstable and when mixed with generalized or primitive

characters tend to disappear. Whether we like to admit it or
not, the result of the mixture of the two races, in the long run,
gives us a race reverting to the more ancient, generalized and
lower type.[5]

Compared with the European influx, Latino immigration to
the United States was limited. From 1906 to 1915 only 127,000 Mexicans sought citizenship, and the new population settled primarily in the Southwest with other Latinos who had become citizens
with the acquisition of lands by the United States after the Mexican-American War and in the Gadsden purchase.

The confusion over racial intermixing in Latino countries,
along with a deeper-rooted Anglo-Saxon prejudice against Europeans of Latin descent, were evident in scouting reports the Reds
had received concerning Almeida's ability and his heritage. One
report read:

> He is a mulatto, speaks fair English. Is very independent and
> worth some money ... has no ginger and nothing to say, and
> also claimed he is not game.[6]

No reports of any sort, before or after this, ever mentioned
rumors that Almeida was of partial African descent. The charac-
terization that Almeida was a mulatto, therefore, seems to have
been based in the scout's preconceptions of Cubans, which must
have included the idea that all Cubans were of mixed ethnic heritage. Another scouting report also demonstrated the preoccupa-
tion with the Cuban's ethnicity:

> I can not give you any figures on Almeida. He is young, a trifle
> above medium height and weighs 155, I would think.
>   Were he a white man, he might be good for the big show. He
> is Cuban, all right, not a nigger. But I find the presence of
> these Cubans breeds discontent here and think it would do so
> even more on a major league club.
>   Like the other Cubans on the team, he is good when they
> are winning, but there is no fight in any of them when they are
> losing.[7]

In both accounts Cubans were seen as inherently lazy and
unwilling to fight when the going got tough. The second report
also characterizes them as malcontents, likely to stir up trouble

among fellow players. The sentence identifying Almeida as a Cuban, "not a nigger," reflected the fear that light-skinned players of African descent would insinuate themselves into organized baseball by denying their African heritage and claiming to be of pure European descent. This ploy would be used by two other Cubans, Roberto Estalella and Tomas de La Cruz. Both men played in the major leagues for brief periods before Jackie Robinson, though it was suspected in Cuba that they were of African descent.[8]

Armando Marsans and Rafael Almeida were not the first Latinos to play in the major leagues. Two foreign-born Latinos and at least one Latino U.S. citizen preceded the two Cubans. Esteban Bellán, also Cuban, played for the Troy Haymakers and the New York Mutuals in the National Association in the early 1870s. Luis Castro was a Colombian utility infielder who played for the World Champion Philadelphia Athletics in 1902. Both men were educated in the United States and perfected their baseball skills in this country. Vincent "Sandy" Nava was born to Cuban parents in San Francisco, California, in 1850. He played for the Providence nine in the National League and for Baltimore in the American Association in the 1880s.

But being permitted to play in the major leagues because they were deemed to be of purely Iberian stock did not guarantee equality for Bellán, Castro, or Nava, nor would it for Marsans and Almeida. Though Western European, the Spaniard was usually lumped by racial theorists with other Mediterranean peoples that carried the stigma of inferiority such as the Italians and the Greeks. Physically, the stereotype of Iberians was of people "marked by relatively short stature, sometimes greatly depressed ... and also by a comparatively light, bony framework and feeble muscular development."[9] The small stature of both Marsans and Almeida's probably served to reinforce the idea that Hispanics were racially inferior.

The ruling class of Spain had descended from Northern European stock, according to one contemporary explanation for smaller statures of Hispanics. These Northern Europeans

> controlled the Spanish states during the endless crusades against the Moors ... but when their blood became impaired by losses in wars waged outside of Spain and in the conquest of the Americas, the scepter fell from this noble race into the

hands of the little, dark Iberian, who had not the physical vigor or the intellectual strength to maintain the world empire built up by the stronger race....
The splendid conquistadors of the New World were of Nordic type, but their pure stock did not long survive their new surroundings and to-day they have vanished utterly, leaving behind them only their language and their religion.[10]

Furthermore, the Spanish Inquisition was believed by some to have affected Spaniards significantly. The Catholic Church condemned an average of 1,000 heretics per year for almost three centuries to the stake or imprisonment. "No better method of eliminating genius producing strains of a nation could be devised and if such were its purpose the result was eminently satisfactory, as is demonstrated by the superstitious and unintelligent Spaniards of today."[11]

Despite current race theories, conditions in the Cincinnati Reds organization in 1911 were uniquely favorable to the signing of Marsans and Almeida. Frank Bancroft, the Reds business manager, had been the first manager to take an American professional team to Cuba when in 1878, he led the Hop Bitters nine on their barnstorming tour to the island and had been impressed by many of the Cuban players.

The Reds, themselves, played a series of games in Cuba in the fall of 1908. In 1909, Bancroft returned to Cuba as business manager of the Philadelphia Athletics. During this trip Bancroft saw Almeida play and was convinced of his qualifications for the National League.[12] Bancroft proposed acquiring him but Reds President August Herrmann was not yet willing to sign Almeida. Thomas Lynch, who had managed Marsans and Almeida in New Britain in 1909, and was now president of the National League, also recommended Almeida and Marsans to Herrmann.

By early June 1911, it was clear the Cincinnati Reds were mired in a disastrous season. Attendance was shrinking rapidly. "The fans have evidently given up hope for which they cannot be blamed..." said the *Cincinnati Enquirer* and those in favor of bringing the Cubans to Cincinnati finally prevailed.[13]

Unlike Jackie Robinson's debut in the major leagues in 1947, an event motivated, in part, by the desire for social justice, the Reds brought Armando Marsans and Rafael Almeida to the big leagues solely as a business move. A trial period of thirty days was negotiated with New Britain. If the players failed to compete successfully at the big league level, or if overwhelming opposition arose against their ethnicity, the players could be sent back to New Britain at the cost of their options alone. If the players made good, and their reception by the National League and the public was favorable, the pair would be purchased at the end of the option period. In either case, it was hoped that the novelty of the first Cubans to play in the major leagues in forty years would be enough to fill at least some of the empty seats in Cincinnati. Marsans and Almeida would also be strong draws in New York, Philadelphia, and Brooklyn, the three National League cities with large Cuban populations. If the signing of these two players brought these Cuban expatriate communities into the ballparks, the visiting team would, under the terms of the National League agreement, share in the windfall.[11]

Signing Marsans and Almeida was not without risks. Their own actions seemed to support the stereotypes of a lack of desire in Latinos. Herrmann knew that Almeida had failed to report to New Britain for the 1911 season, and that Marsans had disappeared back to Cuba in mid–May due to an altercation with his manager or his mother's illness. Whether one accepted the Cubans' excuses or not, the fact is that they were both players who had deserted their minor league team.

The *Cincinnati Post* interpreted these incidents in the patronizing tone of the times, saying that Almeida did not report in 1911 because his feet were sore, and that Marsans quit the team in mid-season because he was in a batting slump. The implication was that the two Cubans were not reliable; they "lacked sand and will never do for the big show."[15]

Why were Marsans and Almeida chosen to be the first Cubans to play in the National League? Luis Padron was still playing in the United States and Alfredo Cabrera was the shortstop on the New Britain team. The most plausible explanation is that Cabrera and Padron were passed over because of their darker complexions.

Though there were no written rules barring players of color, the *Sporting News* pointed out:

...nothing darker than an Indian ever has been tolerated in fast society, [a colloquial reference to the major leagues] and it is not likely that either Marsans or Almeida will be permitted to perform in the big league if it is found that either has African blood in his veins.[16]

Almeida's light skin and thinner, sharper facial features usually had forestalled any questions about his ethnic heritage. In contrast, Marsans's olive skin, full lips, and flat, wide nose suggested to some the possibility of African foreigners.

Guiding the Cubans through the barriers to their integration in the National League would be difficult if doubts about their racial heritage could not be removed. The opposition that the Cubans had witnessed in New Britain was small in comparison to the reaction they could face in Cincinnati. The Reds were a major league team, and therefore, played on the national stage. In New Britain judgment was in the hands of local fans and those of the other teams in the Connecticut League, whereas in Cincinnati the entire sporting public of the United States would have a voice in the issue. Anticipating controversy, August Herrmann wrote one of Cuba's most prominent baseball reporters, the balding, bespectacled Victor Muñoz. On June 17th, he received a telegram in reply:

> August Herrmann,
>   Cincinnati (Ohio)
>   I know personally both parents of our great players Marsans and Almeida and guarantee that none of them have other than pure caucasian blood in their veins, their claim to members of the white race is as good as yours or mine.
>   Victor Muñoz

The enquiry seems to have been as much about putting a favorable spin on the signing as a genuine wish to ascertain the players' ethnicity. The Reds organization supplied information about the factfinding mission to the press, leading the *Cincinnati Times-Star* to report that:

> Mr. Herrmann investigated the families and records of both young men. He found beyond dispute or cavil, that they are well-educated Spaniards of good families.... Both fathers are Spanish-born and there isn't a chance to denominate either of them as chocolate soldiers.[17]

The quality and depth of the investigation are questionable since two important facts were either not discovered or not made public: Marsans and Almeida had toured the United States in 1905 with a racially-mixed Cuban baseball team; and, after several reports of his Spanish heritage, the fact Almeida was actually of Portuguese descent only came to light when Almeida mentioned it. Still, the goal of preventing any official challenge to the eligibility of the two Cubans was achieved.

Native American Mike Balenti also joined the Reds in 1911 from a minor league team in Macon, Georgia. His signing, coupled with the Cubans joining the Reds, sent the press on an excited journey to outdo one another with purportedly humorous coverage of the cosmopolitan make-up of the Reds. "Buffalo Bill's Congress of All Nations has nothing on the Red outfit," reported one paper, adding the hotels where the Reds stayed were printing their menus in seven different languages.[18]

Before 1911, baseball was not homogenous. Players of Irish descent, German-Americans, French, and others loved, played, and succeeded at baseball. There were two groups, however, that fell into the nebulous region on this spectrum between black and white. Though allowed to play in the major leagues, Native Americans and Latinos, were subjected to abuse not experienced by players of Northern European descent. Each group embraced the game and produced stars of the diamond, but they remained haunted by stereotypes.

In the eyes of many whites, Native Americans were the savages of the western plains, mounted on horses, battling the army or settlers. General Custer had ridden into infamy only thirty-five years before Marsans, Almeida, and Balenti played their first game for the Reds. The memory of this event and others in the conflicts between whites and Native Americans were fresh in the collective mind.

The first Native American star was Louis Sockalexis of the Penobscot tribe in Maine. He first played baseball professionally for the team at the Poland Springs resort in Maine where his exceptional talents were quickly noticed. He was recruited to play for the Holy Cross College team, and then, in a time of less rigid collegiate athletic rules, played for the Notre Dame team. He joined the Cleveland Spiders of the National League the following season, reportedly after the Spiders' owner had bailed him out of jail.

Sockalexis's first season with the Spiders in 1897 consisted of sixty-six games. He batted .338 with a .460 slugging average, hitting eight triples and three home runs. But Sockalexis had reputedly begun to sacrifice his talents to alcohol even before the end of that first season and the press disseminated the apocryphal story that Sockalexis's father had paddled his canoe from Maine to Washington, D.C., to ask the president to forbid his son from playing baseball. By the following year, Sockalexis's brilliant star had burnt itself out. He returned to Maine to work as a ferryman and a lumberjack.

John McGraw made one of the most infamous attempts to get past baseball's color barrier in 1901. McGraw held the New York Giants's spring training in Hot Springs, Arkansas, that year. While in camp, McGraw noticed the talents of one of the hotel's bellboys on the baseball diamond. McGraw was so impressed that he wanted the player, Charlie Grant, to join the Giants. There was one major obstacle. Charles Grant was of African descent. McGraw came up with a plan to get past this issue. He created a Native American persona for Grant and named him "Chief Tokahoma." When "Tokahoma's" heritage was questioned, Grant and McGraw both claimed that Tokahoma was half Cherokee Indian. Suspicions mounted among writers and fans and Grant was dropped from the team before they left Arkansas.

Other Native Americans followed Sockalexis to the major leagues and excelled. The Philadelphia Athletics purchased Charles Albert "Chief" Bender in 1903. Bender's mother was a member of the Chippewa tribe, and his father was a German-American settler. Bender pitched in the major leagues for sixteen seasons and was inducted into the Hall of Fame in 1953. His career highlights include leading the American League in winning percentage in 1910, 1911, and 1914, and pitching in five World Series. After his playing career ended, Bender became a coach for the White Sox, the Giants, and the Athletics.

The sobriquet "Chief" was applied to virtually all Native Americans who played in the major leagues. John Tortes Meyers, of the Cahuila tribe in California, was no exception. After he played for three minor league teams, the New York Giants purchased Meyers for the 1909 season, and he quickly became their star catcher. Meyers was not only a great player but he challenged the prevailing stereotype of Native Americans by being well-read and attuned to the political, social, and artistic trends of the day. After his retirement, Meyers made a brief comment that reveals the prejudice Native Americans, and presumably Latinos, faced in baseball. "In those days, when I was young, I was considered a foreigner. I didn't belong. I was an Indian."[19]

Marsans and Almeida stayed in Cincinnati for three days before leaving on a road trip with the Reds that would take them to Chicago, then on a swing through the East. In those three days in Cincinnati, Marsans and Almeida began to endear themselves to many of the writers and fans. Their flashy moves in warm-ups before games were described as "thrilling"[20] and their physical appearance and polite mannerisms caused "the fickle female fans to look on with delight."[21]

In Chicago, on July 4, 1911, three days after joining the Reds, Almeida and Marsans played in their first game in the major leagues. The Reds were losing the first game of a doubleheader 8–1. Both of the Cubans were sent in as pinch hitters in the seventh inning. While Almeida holds claim to being the first Cuban to bat in the twentieth century in the major leagues, the first hit belongs to Marsans; Almeida struck out his first time at bat, while Marsans hit a clean single. In their second chances at the plate it was Almeida who earned a hit, and Marsans who was retired, thrown out at first. A few days after that historic game Reds Manager Clark Griffith wrote to Herrmann on July 8th. He said he was not impressed by Almeida because he was "slow and dead in all his movements and actions" whereas Marsans was "lively and more intelligent."[22] But both men began to see sporadic play: pinch-hitting, pinch-running, making late-game substitutions, and occasionally filling starting roles.

Almeida was the one who first had attracted the attention of the Reds during Frank Bancroft's tour of Cuba. It was Marsans, however, who awed the press in 1911. After two games in New York, the following article appeared:

> Armando Marsans has played very clever ball in all departments. He has looked good in practice all along, and the test of the last two games against the Giants, and before big crowds at the Polo Grounds, has shown him to be a young man with plenty of speed and the good old nerve. He has had little to do in the field, but handles himself like a veteran out there. At the bat he is perfectly at home, and on the bases he has every appearance of being a real, aggressive runner, using judgment along with speed.[23]

The Reds had accurately calculated the appeal of Marsans and Almeida to the Cuban communities in the eastern cities. Hundreds of Cubans flocked to see them in their first games in the East.[24] Before the end of the thirty-day trial, Marsans had earned a permanent place with the Reds. As for Almeida, Herrmann was still undecided and chose to extend his option.[25]

Though Marsans and Almeida won over many fans, reports of how their teammates received them vary. One paper wrote, "Both boys are a credit to the game, and the other players are rooting for them to make good," while another said,

> Marsans and Almeida flock by themselves. The rest of the Reds treat them civilly and politely enough, but do not mix and fraternize with the young Cubans as they should. Possibly the difficulty of carrying on any conversation with the foreigners retards sociability, for the newcomers speak only a little English in a feeble way. Still, it looks as if some effort should be made to make the Cubans feel at home. They are thorough gentlemen, unobtrusive, polished and courteous to a dot.[26]

In New Britain the company of their countrymen had allowed them to live with limited knowledge of English. Now in Cincinnati, Marsans approached English with the same determination he approached baseball. When Marsans stepped to the plate, a small blue dictionary was often visible, peering out from his uniform's hip pocket. One Cincinnati newspaper described Marsans limping after sliding into second base. In the vignette, one of Marsans's teammates asked why Marsans was limping. Marsans responded, "I have slided on my syntax an' ze etymology est have bump me mos' severs!"[27]

This began a trend in reports of Latinos in baseball that would last for decades. Many newspapermen chose to report the dialogue of Marsans, Almeida, and subsequent Latino players phonetically. When written accurately and truthfully, the technique gives the reader a truer glimpse of what it would be like to be with the player. Many reporters, however, began to fictionalize accounts, such as the one above. Some accounts intimated the players' lack of intelligence:

> One of the big biscuit firms has a bakery in Philadelphia with two towers, from each of which flaunts a great red banner with the name of the firms best-known product in white letters. Senor Marsans, [sportswriter Victor] Munōz and Almeida were passing the bakery and studied the flags with much interest.

"Ees mus' be foreign consulate," said Senor Marsans, "but I never see, in my geograph' de map of de nation 'Weneeda.' Mus' be new repub' in Sout' Amerique, si?"[28]

The veracity of these reports is doubtful, but they were printed with no disclaimers. The same newspaper reported:

"I have always unnerstan," said Senor Almeida Wednesday, "dat dees cit' of Boston ees de place where de Engleesh language ees spok' de bes,' de mos' correc'."

"Quite so, Senor," responded Mr. Keefe. "What about it?"

"Why," wailed Senor Almeida, "I see, only dees morn, de sign on de restaurant, on de café, dat say 'Childs.' Now, I not spik mooch of de Eengleesh, but even I know dat ees wrong, dat eet shoul be 'CHILDREN' an' so I wonder dat dey caal dees place so cult' and so refine'."[29]

In another case, two Cuban reporters following baseball in the United States chose opposing teams as favorites to win the World Series. A Cincinnati newspaper reported they "exchanged cards, called for seconds to conduct the duel, and finally agreed the loser of the bet should refrain from conducting or agitating a revolution for five years to come—which, to a Cuban, is some penalty."[30]

On July 27th, Almeida responded to an ovation he received for hitting a double "by doffing his cap in a polite Castilian manner." The formal mannerisms of the Cuban elite were different from what was usual in the United States. The *Cincinnati Enquirer* describes Almeida's gesture as follows: "no mere lifting of the cap goes with the Castilians. They raise their lids far above their heads and make a graceful bow to the populace."[31] Almeida's action calls to mind the moment in Ernest Thayer's "Casey at the Bat" when Casey steps to the plate, "and when responding to the cheers he lightly doffed his cap." The contrast between the two ways of performing the same act is a wonderful illustration of how Cubans had adapted baseball to reflect their society's mannerisms. More importantly, Almeida's action may be seen as the symbolic beginning of Latino influence upon baseball in its native land.

There were moments of disappointment in the euphoria of July 1911. In Marsans's first at bat against the Giants' legendary pitcher Christy Mathewson, he hit a double. But he grounded out when he came to the plate in the top of the ninth with men on second and third, and the Reds down by a score of 4–3.[32] Still, Marsans seemed almost beyond criticism. After one disastrous game, when he was hit by a batted ball, picked off second base with a man on third, and tagged out at first base after a line drive was caught in the 12th inning, one paper reported, "Marsans is an exceedingly clever base runner, and will not make these mistakes again."[33]

Marsans's batting average dropped to .291 in fifty-five at bats. The batting slump was attributed to bad luck: He was the victim of fabulous defensive plays,[34] or hit the ball hard but directly at infielders. Still, he found a starting job, if only temporarily, with the injury of the Reds' rightfielder. By the end of July, Almeida was getting more playing time at third base, but his flaws were more apparent than Marsans's. Reporters thought he was slow throwing the ball after he fielded it,[35] and his range to his left was limited.[36] His offensive worth was never in question; while Marsans beat out infield hits, stole bases, and bunted his way onto base, Almeida was always an impressive power hitter. Almeida's average went as high as .324 and he finished the season with a .312 batting average—the highest among the Reds who had played in more than ten games. Marsans ended with a .261 average, playing in fifty-eight games while stealing eleven bases.

The Reds finished the season with 70 wins versus 83 losses earning them sixth place in the eight-team National League, twenty-three games behind the New York Giants.

The successes of Marsans and Almeida in their first season in the National League forever changed the game of baseball. They proved to the American public, and organized baseball, that Cubans could compete at the highest level of baseball. Articles appeared that spoke of a future including even more Cubans:

> If the Cuban players who are given a chance in the future show they are as capable of holding their own in ability with the players of this country as Marsans and Almeida surely have there will be demand for the foreigners that will not only tend to improve the sport in a department that the evolution of baseball makes necessary for its future progression and further development, but it will also broaden the scope of the game, and when ever that is done it will be a grand, good thing for all countries and peoples.[37]

Several major league teams began to focus on Alfredo Cabrera,

the former teammate of Marsans and Almeida, who was still playing with New Britain. He signed with the Boston Nationals after
the Athletics showed interest, and eventually had a brief stint with
the St. Louis Cardinals.[38] Because Marsans, Almeida, and Cabrera
were exceptionally fast, management began to look at Cuba as a
source of players innately suited to the trend in speed currently
in vogue in baseball.[39] The press and public's inability to see Latino
players as individuals was, and would remain, a primary stumbling
block in the acceptance of Latino players as people rather than as
living stereotypes.

4

Opportunity Seized

The Reds ordered their players to report to Columbus, Georgia, for spring training by March 2, 1912. Marsans sent the following letter (whose level of English hints at a ghost writer) to August Herrmann on February 17th:

Dear Mr. Herrmann:
Your last favor just received and in answer to its contents I beg to say that I am unable to report on the date indicated, the 2d of March. Unaware of the fact that I would have to report so early when I signed my contract to manage the Almendares team, of the local League, made the date of expiration of said document the 15th of March; as you see I am in a very bad fix, because it is my desire to obey your order, and at the same time am unwilling to break my contract with the local club, that have treated me royally. It is a matter that you alone can solve, conferring me a favor that I will appreciate very much, viz: to extend the reporting date to March 15th, that is to say for me to leave Havana that day; the trip from here is a very short one. This delay will not hurt me, because I am playing here regularly and in perfect shape, so it will be a matter of small importance to the club, because I will be able to play with the Reds as soon as I arrive in Columbus and do my best for you and Manager O'Day.

47

Hoping that you will confer me this time another proof of
your kindness, I remain.
Sincerely Yours,
Armando Marsans[1]

A letter from the acting president of the Almendares Baseball Club arrived on Herrmann's desk soon after Marsans's. The
letter said Marsans had not realized that the contract with Almendares extended to the 30th of March, not the 15th and that Almendares was currently in position to win the league pennant.
Herrmann conceded to the request, extending Marsans's reporting date to March 15th.[2]

Hank O'Day replaced Clark Griffith as the manager of the
Cincinnati Reds for the 1912 season. O'Day was tall with slightly
stooped, broad shoulders. He was a stern adherent to discipline
with "little oratorical ability"[3] and an eccentric means of dress; he
was once seen in a suit described as "elephant breath gray, with
checkers in the pattern and a wistful coat-tail."[4] O'Day had been
an umpire in the major leagues for several years and a player for
seven seasons prior to that. The Cincinnati Reds management
believed his extensive experience as an umpire qualified him for
the position of manager.

O'Day pushed his men in spring training, but also reigned
them. He walked the foul lines watching the players, taking a
patient view of the five-week training session. "Every year I have
seen brilliant players returned to the minors who should by all
rights be kept in the big show," he said. "Some of them haven't
been given a fair show with the majors, while still others have been
hurt in the practice games and will not tell their manager of their
injuries. For these reasons I am determined to hang onto the boys
until I know their ability. Some of them are showing up splendidly
right now, while others are naturally slow in coming around and
will be all right in a few days."[5]

Baseball was, by the standards of the day, an egalitarian institution, drawing from all segments of white American culture.
Eddie Grant, out to prove he was a better hitter than his .223 batting average in 1911 showed, boasted a Harvard diploma. In contrast, Murphy, a newly-recruited catcher, previously with the Dallas
club in the Texas League, had spent the winter working as a miner
to support his brother, who had recently broken both legs in an
accident in the mines.

"Long" Larry McLean was one of the hardest workers on the squad, though the veteran catcher had apparently had a relaxing off-season and began spring training weighing 228 pounds. He wore a rubber shirt during the workouts to help him lose twenty excess pounds. Bob Bescher was one of the fastest men in all of baseball, with an intuitive sense for base running. He had won the base stealing title in the National League in 1909, 1910 and 1911. For now he was hampered by a nagging injury he had suffered three years previously, when he broke his ankle turning to chase a fly ball.

The recruits were reminded of their precarious positions with the team when they saw the scout from the New York Highlanders of the American League watching them in practice. The scout took notes on the young players, hoping to find a jewel among those the Reds would discard.[6]

The regular outfielders from the 1911 season were Bescher, Johnny Bates, and Mike Mitchell. The three players were certain to retain their positions for the upcoming season, leaving Marsans to battle Elmer Miller for the position of substitute outfielder.

The Cuban had the edge on Miller in several departments: Marsans was a versatile player, able to play any of the three outfield positions, and also a skilled first baseman; he was in superlative shape from playing all winter in Cuba; and he had proven himself in the 1911 season. Though Miller was also very fast, the Cuban impressed O'Day from the moment he arrived in camp—late, as usual, after the typical confusion about his travel plans. Elmer Miller was fighting a losing battle.

Rafael Almeida was still not in camp by March 12th, 1912, the last day the players could report without a fine. Victor Muñoz, newspaper correspondent from Havana, arrived on March 20th. He had expected to find Almeida on his ship with him from Havana and was surprised the wayward Cuban was not aboard. Almeida was still not in camp on the 20th, eighteen days after the date he was to report.

The weather warmed into the eighties toward the end of camp and the team showed how they had progressed under O'Day. The veterans took turns at batting practice, driving the incoming pitches around the field. After an hour, it was the recruits' and substitutes' turn at bat. Marsans batted in this second group. He displayed his sharpened eye and aggressiveness at bat. Marsans was as fit as any of the Reds players and made a strong case to be named the first replacement outfielder.

On the 23rd of March, the Reds closed camp in Columbus. They had scheduled several games with minor league teams along their route back to Cincinnati. The first stop was Birmingham, Alabama; the second was to be Montgomery, but the field was too wet for their game and the players anxiously loitered around the hotel, playing cards and billiards.

The bad weather followed the Reds as they made their way to Cincinnati. After squeezing in one game in Chattanooga, rain caused the cancellation of the second game and the morning practice the next day. Marsans received his first opportunity as a starter when a wild pitch struck Mike Mitchell in the head (batters did not wear helmets in 1912). The beaning forced Mitchell to sit out eight games, giving Marsans his first chance to show what he could do with consistent playing time.

After one last practice in Chattanooga on the morning of April 3, the Reds boarded the 9:45 evening train and left the South. Due to a four-hour delay on the trip, they arrived in Cincinnati at 10:30 A.M., which meant that the game in Columbus, Ohio, planned for that afternoon had to be postponed. A loyal group of fans greeted the Reds' train, cheering as the tanned, fit players stepped down from their Pullman.

Thirteen players went to Columbus on the morning train the next day where two thousand people came to watch the Reds' five to three victory over the local minor-league team. Still substituting for Mitchell, Marsans covered himself with "glory and distinction."[7] The Cuban earned first base beating out a bunt and subsequently scored. In the eighth, Marsans was walked after ending up on the ground evading a wild pitch. He stole second, took third on a throwing error, and Miller brought him home with a clean single.

Marsans's play as Mitchell's replacement drew favorable reviews:

> Every time Marsans gets on base, he springs something which shows him to be not only fast, but very smart and foxy. He overlooks no chance to advance, keeps his eye on the ball, is seldom caught napping, and is, in fact, one of the best base-runners on the team. No slouch of a hitter, either, and in the field he is as good as they make them.[8]

Almeida still had not rejoined the Reds, though he was supposed to have reported for training in Georgia on March 12. A telegram promised he would arrive in Cincinnati on April 1st. But Almeida did not fulfill his promise. Another letter, which offered no explanation for his month-long delay, said Almeida would leave Cuba in time to meet the Reds in Cincinnati when they returned from Columbus, Ohio.

This 1912 caricature of Rafael Almeida illustrates some of the stereotypes the early Cuban players faced.

On April 6, Almeida finally arrived in Cincinnati and went directly to meet with O'Day. Almeida explained that his month-long delay was due to a lawsuit having dragged on, but O'Day was less than sympathetic. The previous day the Reds had asked for waivers on Almeida, meaning that they asked all National League teams not to sign Almeida so that he could be demoted to the minor leagues with the Reds still retaining their rights to him. All teams complied and the Reds were free to demote Almeida when they pleased. Almeida's talent was revered in Cuba, but he carried with him the reputation of unfulfilled potential. Spurred on by criticism from his friends in Cuba, he wanted to shed his reputation for shiftlessness. Almeida had resolved to prove what he could do if he were to focus on baseball.[9] But his tardiness in reporting angered the Reds and the threat of demotion was their last resort. Though the Reds could have demoted Almeida to the minor leagues at that time, they chose to keep him on the team.

Before the first regular season game of 1912, the Reds received an offer for both Marsans and Almeida. Clark Griffith, who had managed the Reds in 1911, wanted the Cubans on his new team, the Washington Senators.[10] The Boston Nationals, who had been interested in Almeida since his time in New Britain, also made Herrmann an offer for Almeida, but both offers were rejected.[11]

April 11th was opening day of the 1912 season. Cafes and cigar stores sent contingents of loyal patrons to the new ballpark in chartered streetcars and horse-drawn carriages. They were joined by the "Thrifty Crowd," who earned their name by depositing a quarter each week from the first of the year with a shop owner. In exchange, they were treated to a reserved seat, dinner, and popcorn and soda. The sixteen "fanesses" of the Ladies' Enterprise Bowling Club headed the parade of automobiles from the Enterprise Bowling Alley. The sell-out crowd of more than 27,000 carried cameras, opera glasses, and cushions. They passed Herman Ritt, known to faithful fans from years past, standing in his elevated booth near the entrance hawking scorecards. The fans entered the stadium through ten-foot-wide entrances in the brick façade, which was accentuated with light-toned false columns and arches over the windows.

Two hours before the game began, the right field pavilion was already full, but the left field pavilion still showed empty seats. The crowd was allowed to cross the field to even the balance. Many of the fans from the bleachers sneaked onto the field in the tumult, and claimed a fifty-cent pavilion seat for the price of their twenty-five-cent bleacher ticket.

The new field was large by the standards of the day, and immense in comparison to the fields of the late 20th century. The largest of any of the major league parks, it measured 420 feet from home plate to the wall in center field, and 360 feet from home plate to the fences down the foul lines.[12] The field was asymmetrical, with a vast left-centerfield. The plate was ninety feet from the backstop, allowing plenty of room for catchers to field foul pop-ups. This generous space also allowed wild pitches and passed balls to rattle around behind the catcher while base runners advanced easily.

Instead of stairs, which slowed the crowds, the stadium featured a relatively new system of ramps leading from street level to the first level. Twelve more ramps led from the first level to the second deck. Two hundred and nineteen reserved boxes, in the front rows of both the decks of the grandstand, provided seating for six to ten people each, with rows of enameled green steel chairs with slatted wood seats behind them.[13] Telephones, messenger and cab service stations, as well as cafes, were located throughout the park. Much was made of the "Women's retiring rooms," located on both levels of the grandstand, under the attentive watch of a team of maids.[14]

The grandstand formed an open, two-deck horseshoe around the diamond, extending just beyond first and third base. Single level pavilions stretched from there to the foul poles in left and right field. Sandwiched between the outfield fence in right field and Western Avenue were the bleachers.

The structure that cupped the infield contained the offices of the Reds management. There was a clubroom for the players, above the offices, furnished with a pool table and the leading magazines and newspapers of the day. Manager O'Day's desk was in one corner of the room.[15] The new facility cost $400,000. It was praised by all as one of the best baseball parks in the world.

On opening day, the new home of the Reds had no name. Many in Cincinnati felt it would have been an appropriate honor to name the stadium after Reds President August Herrmann but Herrmann declined to do so. He later decided to christen the stadium Redland Field. This same building would evolve into Cincinnati's Crosley Field.

At 2 o'clock the Reds emerged from their dressing room to

an extended ovation. The Chicago Cubs, in their dark blue road uniforms, soon joined them on the field and the ordered chaos that is a pre-game warm-up began. Men stood on the sidelines, tossing balls lightly, doing calisthenics, and running short sprints. Then they spread out like ants from their nest and occupied the field, running to catch fly balls or sidling like crabs on the infield, fielding grounders. Each player took batting practice while the pitchers continued to warm up along the foul lines. The dirt of the infield and the bluish-green Kentucky bluegrass sod set off the bright new uniforms of the players.

Vendors in the stands hawked their goods. Around the infield Cincinnati's elite visited one another in their reserved boxes, men in suits and women in their best dresses and large hats.

The opposing teams gathered at home plate as game time approached, and paraded out to the flagpole in center field with Weber's Marching Band in the lead. Hank O'Day, clad in a new suit and light gray fedora, led the Reds. O'Day and the Cubs manager raised the twelve-by-twenty-four-foot American flag and the teams returned to home plate. Admiring fans presented O'Day with a bouquet of carnations. Then the two teams proceeded to August Herrmann's box where the mayor of Cincinnati stood. With brevity and eloquence he opened the season saying, in part:

> To you, ballplayers, I need say very little. We take delight in your skill, your fleetness and your knowledge of the great American game ... the American people love the winner much, but fair play and sportsmanlike conduct, more, is necessary. Your reputation and popularity attest that you are already ardent believers in the sentiment.[16]

The Cubs were a potent opening-day competitor. Frank Chance, known as the "Peerless Leader," was their manager. He was the last stop for the ball in the legendary Tinker-to-Evers-to-Chance double play combination, immortalized in Franklin P. Adams's poem. Each member of the trio would end up in Cooperstown among the pantheon of baseball greats. The outfield was strong defensively, and a concern for opposing pitchers. Frank "Wildfire" Schulte, in right field, led the league in 1911 with twenty-one home runs, also driving in 107 runs. He received an automobile for winning the Chalmers Award, given to the league's most valuable player that year.

The announcer yelled the lineups through a brass bullhorn,

his voice barely audible over the excitement of the fans. The umpire shouted "Play Ball!" and the season began. The Reds scored a run in their half of the first inning. Chicago answered with five runs in the third inning. The Reds' six run response in the fourth inning was decisive. The game ended with the Reds winning 10–6. Four balls were hit into the overflow crowds permitted to sit on the grass behind the outfielders. The umpires and managers had discussed this possibility before the game. They agreed that three bases would be allotted to the batter. Marsans, playing in right field for Mitchell, had one hit in four plate appearances. He drove in a run with that hit and also earned a sacrifice. He was credited with one put out for catching a fly ball and one assist for throwing out a runner.

The Reds swept the two-game series with the Cubs and Marsans showed that he was more than just a utility outfielder. On April 14th, Marsans had two hits in four plate appearances. He scored in the fourth and drove in two runs with a bases-loaded double in the seventh. Marsans's place in the lineup was, at least temporarily, assured by superstition, as well as by Mitchell's lingering dizziness; according to baseball tradition, O'Day was not going to disturb a winning lineup.

The Reds took four out of their first five games in Cincinnati before heading to Chicago for another series with the Cubs. Managers pay a great deal of attention to batting orders, and O'Day had his well set. Batting first for the Reds was Bob Bescher, whose speed made him the obvious lead-off man. Bescher did not have as high a batting average as some other Reds, nor as many walks, but having him on base with no one ahead of him meant that he could use his speed to rattle a pitcher. His swift running also reduced the chance of a double play. Johnny Bates batted second. He could advance Bescher with a hit-and-run play or was capable of beating out the bunt or infield hit.

Dick Hoblitzell, playing first base, batted third. He had the power to bring Bates or Bescher home with an extra base drive. He was also a good situational hitter, someone who knew where and how to hit a ball tactically. With a man on second and no outs, for example, it is vital that the batter get the runner to third so he can score more easily. Hitting a ground ball, or a fly, to the left side of the field, allows the defense to hold the runner at second base because the ball is fielded close to third base. A ball hit to the right side of the diamond is behind the runner and farther from third. Even if cleanly fielded by the first or second baseman, the defense usually does not risk a throw to third base, instead making the sure out at first base. Hoblitzell proved his ability and knowledge by driving in twelve runs in the first twelve games of the season.

Returning from his injury, Mike Mitchell batted fourth. Known as the "clean-up" position in the batting order, the slot requires someone with power to score players on base. Dick Egan batted fifth, and Arthur Phelan sixth. Phelan was talented enough to bat higher in the order on another team, but early in 1912, the Reds top five were hitting too well for him to be given the opportunity.

Jimmy Esmond and "Harvard" Eddie Grant were both low in the order. Esmond, like Phelan, was a good batsman, but not skilled enough to be placed higher in the Reds' talented batting order. Grant had had a bad season in 1911 and O'Day was still watching to see if he could regain his form. Whoever was catching, Larry McLean or Hank Severeid, batted eighth. Traditionally, catchers were not offensively strong. They were expected to focus on the defensive side of the game, and any offense they could supply would be a bonus. Pitchers, who are almost always the weakest batters on the team, usually batted ninth.

The *Cincinnati Times-Star* reported that "Armando Marsans seems to fit in anywhere on the list and to work his whanging bat with equal skill and success, no matter where he may be asked to work."[17] When Mike Mitchell was ready to return, threatening to remove Marsans from the lineup, outfielder Johnny Bates injured his finger, opening another spot for the Cuban.

On April 21st, Mitchell and Bates were both healthy and in the game, and Marsans was out of the Reds' lineup for the first time in the 1912 season. Marsans had batted .317 in the nine regular season games he started. His thirteen hits in forty-one at bats comprised ten singles, two doubles, and a triple with five stolen bases.

Rafael Almeida was having a harder time than Marsans finding a place in the lineup. His off-field behavior continued to create problems. Leaving for a road trip in late April, Almeida boarded the train, put his baggage down, and asked the porter to make up his berth then went out to buy a cigar and never returned to the Pullman.

"I am positive that Almeida missed the train by accident," said

O'Day, "and I won't even dock him a day's pay; but I wish he'd learn that trains and baseball schedules wait for no man."[18] O'Day's view changed when he did not hear from Almeida the day after he missed the train. The Cincinnati papers began to speculate that Almeida's time with the Reds would soon be over.

Despite Almeida's promise to his Cuban friends to dedicate himself to baseball, his reputation for laziness grew. He was now seen as "not amenable to discipline and ... wholly without ambition."[19] He returned to Cincinnati from St. Louis with the team amid rumors of a trade that would send him to Philadelphia. The Reds, however, thought too much of Almeida's ability to send him to a competing team so on May 8th, they announced that he had been sold to the Birmingham club of the Southern League, but with an option that meant no major league team could acquire him without the Reds' consent. The *Cincinnati Tribune* considered that "With the Southern League Almeida should be a wonder, for he is a hard and natural hitter, fast on the bases, and his fielding should show improvement. He has never known a great desire to shine as a player while with the Redlegs but now that he has been turned adrift by the local club, he will awaken and see the folly of his ways, and get out and hustle to get back in the 'big show.'"[20]

On May 7th, Marsans was put in as a pinch-hitter in the seventh inning of the game. When the Cuban walked to the plate he was greeted with prolonged applause from the crowd, which on that day included William Taft, president of the United States. The knowledgeable fans of Cincinnati were giving Marsans thanks and encouragement for his contributions to the team on their recent road trip. Marsans received a walk that time at bat.[21] The Cincinnati fans singled out Marsans again on the 18th of May, applauding him vociferously for his hard work as he trotted from the dugout to take his place in left field during warm-ups.[22]

The Reds were a half a game behind the first-place New York Giants in the National League at that time. The new stadium and the Reds' early success combined to set records for attendance in Cincinnati; by the end of April, 40 percent of the Reds' average annual attendance had come to the park.[23]

First baseman Dick Hoblitzell was given permission to miss the game on the 23rd of May in order to receive his diploma from the Cincinnati Dental College. It was a much-needed break for the large first baseman. He had been playing with two injured legs, which both had to be tightly bandaged before each game.[24] Marsans played first base for several games and showed his versatility on defense, fielding without error the position that he frequently played in Cuba.[25]

Marsans received the highest compliment in comparison to Ty Cobb in the *Cincinnati Enquirer*:

> If a man shows a tendency to slowness or inaccuracy Cobb makes a mental note of the fact and the next time he hits to that field he is likely to take an extra base. Cobb excels all other players not so much in speed but in brains and powers of observation. While most athletes play a fairly conservative and mechanical game, Cobb is always pulling something and getting away with it that no one else would attempt. His work ... is not so reckless as it looks, because he has the dope on opposing players. Marsans, of the Reds, is a clever baserunner of the Cobb type. The Cuban is very aggressive and yet does not take many foolish chances. He secured a double in one of the Giant games last week, which showed his method. He singled sharply to right field, and, as he always does, came down to first at full speed and made the turn fast. He saw that Becker out in right had juggled the ball for just a fraction of a second in picking it off the ground. Marsans felt that the fraction of a second combined with the necessary hurried throw would get him to secondbase so he kept right on going. He had figured right and made the base easily. It is surprising that there is not more of this kind of stuff pulled off, but the average runner is afraid to take the chance.[26]

On May 30, the *Cincinnati Times-Star* was the first newspaper to refer to Marsans as a star. The article, under the headline "Four Star Players for Three Positions," posed the question of what Manager O'Day should do with the four talented outfielders on his team. The article suggested Marsans should replace Mike Mitchell, the captain of the Reds, who was in a slump and being booed by fans who were unaware the outfielder was playing with an injured right arm. Because Marsans was already substituting for the injured Bates, Mitchell felt he had to play through his injury. Finally, Mitchell announced he would cede his place to Marsans when Bates returned to the lineup.

Marsans, taking Mitchell's place in the outfield, batted in the second position behind Bob Bescher. The two frequently worked the hit and run with success. When Bescher reached first, a signal would be exchanged between the players when the count favored a pitch over the plate. Bescher would run toward second as the pitcher delivered the pitch. Either the second baseman or the shortstop would leave his position and cover second base to receive the throw from the catcher to tag out Bescher. This would open up a hole in the infield, which Marsans could try to hit through.

In mid–June, Marsans was hit on the heel by a pitched ball and received a deep bruise. The injury seemed to limit his speed, but O'Day did not want to take him out of the lineup because he was playing so well.[27] But the pain persisted, and Marsans was finally taken out of the lineup for the second game of a doubleheader on the 4th of July, the first anniversary of his debut with the Reds.

Marsans was so potent on offense that special defenses were employed against him. Most of Marsans's hits were to left field, so opposing teams shifted players around the field to overload the

A portrait of Marsans from 1912 with a diagram illustrating the shifted defense unsuccessfully used against Marsans's potent bat.

left side, leaving the right side relatively open. To assure Marsans would hit into their defensive strength, pitchers were pitching to him almost exclusively on the inside of the plate. It is very difficult for a right-handed hitter to hit an inside pitch to right field. But Marsans continued to reach base. He hit balls through the left side of the shifted infield, he hit balls just over the reach of the infielders that dropped in front of the outfielders, and he hit what few pitches he got on the outside part of the plate into right field.

The Reds continued to play well, and win, but concern about their primary weakness began to grow. None of the pitching recruits whom the Reds had invited to spring training proved to be a real discovery. The problem became more acute when injuries began to mount among the pitchers. In one eight-game stretch the Reds won only once, and gave up at least four runs in eight of the nine games. Pitching continued to be a liability through July, and the Reds' offense also slumped. On the rare occasions when a pitcher had a good game, the offense was unproductive.

The Reds' record suffered. Desperation crept into the management and the team. The tension that builds when a team starts to lose finally erupted. At the end of June, Dick Hoblitzell, at first base, ran to his right to field a ground ball. He cut in front of the second baseman and could not make the play. At the end of the half inning, Manager O'Day, waiting for Hoblitzell in the dugout, chastised him for the bad play. O'Day accused him of making bad plays on other ground balls. Hoblitzell argued back. When Hoblitzell, who was second to bat, went to the plate, he turned and spat one last comment at O'Day. O'Day called him back to the bench and put Severeid in to bat for him. Hoblitzell left the bench, went to the clubhouse, got dressed and left the grounds.[28]

Hoblitzell and Bates were batting below .300 for the first time all season. Bescher's average plummeted and Phelan struggled at the plate. Only Marsans remained consistent, but as the *Cincinnati Times-Star* reported after a loss, "Marsans hit hard, and stole bases, and caught flies, but one man cannot make up for the failure of a whole ball club."[29]

While the Reds continued to sink the press continued its praise of Marsans. On July 18th, the *Commercial Tribune* titled an article "Marsans, the Cuban Player, Is Star of Cincinnati Team This Year." The Cuban was batting .335, the highest among the Reds regulars. Marsans was very active in the batter's box. Never standing still, the Cuban distracted pitchers with his constant motion.

In an article titled "Marsans Rated Best All-Around Star Since Joe Jackson Broke into the Majors," a Philadelphia pitcher explained:

> I'd rather pitch to almost any man in the league than the Cuban in a pinch. He dances around the batter's box so you can never tell when or where he is liable to hit; he has a good eye and makes a pitcher get the ball over. I hate to look up and see Marsans on the bases. He's dangerous on the paths.[30]

"He Is Leading the Reds in Batting" was the title of the following article:

> Armando Marsans, the Cuban outfielder of the Reds, has become one of the most popular players on the circuit through his grand work this summer. Marsans is one of the strongest, safest batsmen that ever wore the red, and a splendid outfielder besides.... He is fast acquiring a good working knowledge of the English language, and is well liked by all those who have met him.[31]

The shifted defense and pitching inside to Marsans had proven ineffective. Word circulated among the pitchers in the league that he could hit pitches on the inside of the plate well so they began to pitch him outside. The Cuban was able to adapt, and the majority of his hits were now going to right field.[32] Marsans was frequently using an old technique that had not been seen recently in the major leagues. To increase his ability to put the ball in play, Marsans, especially on hit and run plays, extended his arms rigidly, instead of swinging at the pitch. Marsans used the technique effectively to drop the ball past the infielders but in front of the outfielders.[33]

Despite his successes, Marsans was still learning. On June 17th, he was touched out by the fielder as he took his lead from third base. The third baseman had caught a foul ball from the previous batter and walked back to his position, hiding the ball in his glove. Both Marsans and the Reds' third base coach assumed he had thrown the ball to the pitcher. Marsans jogged back to the dugout visibly humiliated by his lapse in focus.[34]

What may have been Marsans's worst mistake came on September 2nd. His long drive to right field found the outfield wall by the foul pole and rattled around in the corner. Marsans easily rounded the bases, touching home plate without a slide. But the opponents threw the ball to the third baseman, who stepped on the base. The umpire called Marsans out for having failed to touch third base, nullifying the run.[35]

At least one writer wrote about Marsans's shortcomings:

> Senor Armando must be classed as a regular member of the team, it would be absurd to lay him off in favor of anyone hitting far shy of the Cuban's average. He is a grand ball player, but still lacking the headwork that is needed for a real top-notcher. Sad, but true the good Hidalgo blunders on the bases ever and anon, and is guilty of semi-occasional bones, all of which can be forgiven in consideration of the hits he makes and the catches that he gathers.[36]

In the game on July 27, Marsans charged a low line drive from his outfield position but could not reach it. The ball shot past him and went to the fence. The batter made it all the way around the bases, scoring on an inside-the-park home run. Instead of criticism, Marsans received praise for the play. "It is the sort of progressive playing which wins in the long run.... The percentage is all in favor of the hustler like Marsans, as against the conservative player who never tries for the difficult chances."[37]

Despite Marsans's ability and growing renown, the Reds continued to struggle and dropped out of the "first division," meaning the top half of the League. Many in Cincinnati were beginning to question O'Day's managerial ability and there was open talk about replacing him. In early August, the Cincinnati police reported that a 16-year-old boy had been stabbed after an argument in which he had defended Hank O'Day as manager.[38]

As is typical of losing teams, rumors about trades that would send Cincinnati players to other teams surrounded the Reds. On the 26th of July, the *Cincinnati Post* sports page headline read, "Marsans Will Not Figure in Any Trade Red President Says." "I might as well break up the whole club as trade Marsans," said Herrmann, "I don't believe I would trade him for anybody."[39] Marsans's .341 average ranked seventh in the National League in batting, and he would climb as high as fourth before the end of the season.

Marsans's play endeared him to his countrymen living in the United States. "They turn out in droves to cheer him on, and whenever he comes to bat, a chorus of Spanish war cries rings along the stand. If he makes a hit—as he has quite a habit of doing—the Cubans go plumb dotty, and pretty nearly scratch the concrete off the stand walls."[40]

On August 3rd, the Reds faced the New York Giants, with the inimitable Christy Mathewson on the mound. Marsans hit three singles and a double against one of baseball's greatest pitchers. One of the singles was an infield hit, which Marsans was praised for having beaten out instead of giving up when he saw the ball had been fielded.[41] He received loud applause from the many Cubans in the stands and also from a contingent from New Britain that had come to watch their former player. John McGraw, the Giants' manager, was quoted as saying, "If there's any more like him in Cuba, I'll take them in a minute."[42]

Meanwhile, Rafael Almeida was leading the Southern League with a .419 average in mid–July. "Two and three hits game after game, with doubles, triples, and stolen bases ad libitum. The Marquis of Habana has evidently waked up to a sense of his obligations and his baseball duties," wrote one reporter.[43] His performance attracted several offers from major league teams but August Herrmann refused to trade him.

Herrmann would eventually recall Almeida and he rejoined the Reds in New York on September 18. He had slumped in his final weeks with Birmingham but on September 19, Almeida again found himself on a big league field, playing in the second game of a doubleheader. He did not get a hit against Christy Mathewson but did receive a walk and scored a run. Art Phelan, the starting third baseman, came down with a sore throat, allowing Almeida to play regularly at third base. He performed well and assured a place on the Reds' roster for 1913.

Back in Cuba, the City Council of Havana, as enthralled by Marsans's play as the rest of Cuba, decided to award him a gold medal "in recognition of his good hitting with the Cincinnati Reds and the good name he has given Cuba in the baseball world." The medal was to be presented in a ceremony in Havana when Marsans, now called "Cuba's greatest baseball player," returned to Cuba.[44] He arrived in Cuba sooner than expected.

On September 7, Marsans slid into first base, tucking his right leg under him and extending his left leg. As his momentum carried him past the base, his metal cleats snagged in the canvas first base bag. Marsans could not free his foot and twisted his left knee badly. Sliding into first base is frowned upon in baseball not only because running through the base is faster but also because so many injuries result from the play. Marsans had to be helped back to the bench. At first it was thought he would miss only a few days, but soon the doctors determined that he had strained the tendons in his knee and he would not be able to play for the rest of the season. Marsans was granted permission from Herrmann to return to Cuba with about three weeks remaining in the season.

Marsans's departure, hobbling on a cane, was front-page news in Cincinnati. "My stay in the Queen City of Ohio has been very pleasant and I am sad to leave. I have been treated splendidly and I am above all grateful to the fans for their displays of affection of which I have been the object. What's more, President Herrmann and Manager O'Day have been very kind to me...."[45] With those words Marsans left Cincinnati and his 1912 season ended. He returned to Cuba on the *Mascotte* and was greeted at Havana's docks by his brothers and the mob of Cubans.

5

1913

At the end of 1912, reports arrived in Cincinnati claiming that Armando Marsans was dissatisfied with the contract the Reds were offering him for the 1913 season and would hold out. The specific reason was unclear. One report said he wanted a multi-year contract, while others believed he wanted more money. When Marsans, in Cuba for the winter, became aware of the reports, he wrote to August Herrmann:

Dear Mr. Herrmann:-
In a story published by the "Enquirer," it is said that I am a "hold-out" and I want to explain that this is far from the truth, because I will never be such against a man that treated me so kindly always as you did and for whom I will give my best services during my career, as long as these be considered of any value.

I don't know where the "Enquirer" got that piece of news, because I have not said a word to that effect. The only objection to my 1913 contract is that I think it would have been more in accordance with the average salary of regular players to fix mine at $3,600; but if you don't agree with me in this small raise, I am ready to sign it as soon as you send me word to that effect. This is very different of a "hold-out"; my petition is a matter of form more than anything else. Never the less if for

any reason, or without any, you feel opposed to it, please write
to me and I will sign the contract without hesitation, and be
ready to give you and the Club my best services next season just
the same.

Hoping to hear from you, I remain,

Yours sincerely,

Armando Marsans[1]

The Reds had paid Marsans $2400 for the 1912 season. The
first contract they sent him for the 1913 season had stipulated a
salary of $3200. Herrman responded to Marsans's letter on the 13th:

My Dear Mr. Marsans:-
    Your letter of January 5th just received. I am very much
pleased with your letter. I do not know how the Enquirer got
the story they published, but I am sure they did not intend anything wrong. Probably someone cabled them from Havana.
    I thought that the increase of 33% was a very fair one, but
since you are also fair in the matter, I have made up my mind
to pay you $3,400 for next season, which will be a compromise
figure. I sincerely trust that your playing will be of such a character that the Club will be warranted in making another
increase in 1914. Enclosed find new contract, which kindly sign
and return at once.

Respectfully,

August Herrmann[2]

The Reds had finished fourth in the National League in 1912,
regaining their coveted place in the "first division," an improvement of two positions over the previous season. Hank O'Day was
given favorable reviews by the press, and the general opinion was
that he would return for the 1913 season. But Herrmann decided
to replace O'Day with Joe Tinker, perhaps still blaming him for
the mid-season slump that cost the Reds a chance at the pennant.
Joe Tinker was Cincinnati's third manager in Marsans's three seasons with the team. Though there were exceptions, in that era it
was generally the teams that developed continuity that realized
their full potential and won pennants. The annual change in leadership that Marsans and his teammates experienced made this
difficult; with each new manager came a new leadership style, a
new view of the game, and new interpersonal relationships, all
amounting to a constant state of flux.
    Tinker had joined the Chicago Cubs for the 1902 season and

they converted him, against his will, into their shortstop. He reportedly was not popular among his teammates. On the Chicago Cubs team, he had "the least number of friends of any of the players."[3] Though he played next to Johnny Evers for eleven seasons as the Cubs' middle infield—as recorded in Adams's poem—he did not speak to his teammate for years after an argument about a cab ride.

Tinker led the Reds to Mobile, Alabama, for spring training. Bad weather hounded the team, with rain and cold temperatures impeding training. By the 7th of March, only five men signed by the Reds were still missing from training camp, three of them Cuban: Marsans, Almeida, and Tomás Romanach. Romanach was a shortstop touted by players who had played against him in Cuba as being superior to Almeida. He was, in fact, outhitting Almeida in the Cuban league that season. Marsans had recommended Romanach to the Reds, calling him the best of the Cuban infielders, and it was Marsans's influence that made Romanach sign with Cincinnati instead of one of the four other major league clubs that were interested in him.[4]

Marsans's absence from training camp concerned Herrmann. He had wired the Cuban in Havana on March 6th, attempting to learn of his whereabouts. Marsans cabled back saying a letter, written March 2nd, explaining his situation was en route:

> Dear Mr Herrmann:
>
> I had the intention to leave here for the training camp on the date you ordered, but the cigar business in which I placed all my savings, don't let me to leave this City before the 20th; it is a matter of vital importance for me, because I have to leave some one in charge who can attend my interest and my father, who was to be here on the 1st, to take care of it, was retained at Pinar del Rio longer of what he thought he would, promising me to come on the 20th; therefore I am marooned here, against my will, until said date. But I am in perfect shape, because I am playing a little twice a week I am sure that if you give consent to it, I will be ready to give the Club my best services since the day I report to manager Tinker. So I request permission to sail from here to the training camp on the 20th. I hope you will explain the situation to manager Tinker and that he will agree to accede to my request, taking in considerations the above mentioned reasons for it; you can assure him that I am anxious to make up for this little delay in reporting, working to the best of my ability, since the day I shall join the Club.

Hoping to hear from you, I remain
Yours Sincerely,
Armando Marsans[5]

Rafael Almeida had requested permission to report to spring training in Mobile on March 12th.[6] Herrmann granted Almeida this exemption. Tinker wrote Herrmann, "It is a very bad thing to allow players to be late in reporting as it is not fair to the others and if I should have anything to do with it next spring, it will cost the late one some money."[7]

"Manager Tinker is not very much pleased to think that the boys, knowing how important the National League race is to the Cincinnati Club, should stay over in Cuba for a few spring games there after playing all winter and should pay no attention to instructions of himself and President Herrmann to report here with the balance of the players."[8] Tinker wired on the 7th to Havana. He received a response from Almeida saying he would report on March 11th.

Unaware of Marsans's letter to Herrmann, Tinker tried to contact Marsans in Havana without success. Tinker concluded Marsans and Romanach were on their way to Mobile. On the 9th, Herrmann notified Tinker about Marsans letter saying the Cuban could not leave his cigar factory until the 20th. Tinker wired Marsans telling him to report to camp at once. "Tinker has no use for that manana spirit and he intends to give the semi-tropical Reds a taste of discipline."[9]

By the 12th, Tinker was considering benching the recalcitrant Marsans upon his arrival. "It is not that he is in great need of practice that makes the Reds leader sore, but that he is showing the same disregard as the other Cubans for the instructions of the officials of the club. Nearly all the Cubans have failed to realize what an important business baseball is in this country and how essential it is for them to obey orders coming from the manager or President of their club."[10]

Marsans finally declared he would sail from Havana on March 17th with Romanach.[11] Almeida wired Tinker that he, too, would leave with Marsans from Havana.[12] Almeida's failure to report to camp was again jeopardizing his place on the Reds roster. "As for Almeida, he has been a 'tomorrow' fellow and it is apparent that his self-caused banishment to the minors last season did not teach him the value of obedience to the rules of the club in the training camp and during the season."[13]

Marsans and Almeida, arrived in the United States on March 19th, landing in Jacksonville, where they spent the day. Romanach, who spoke no English, had changed his mind at the last minute and did not sail north with Marsans and Almeida to report to the Reds, apparently too intimidated by the life in the United States without English.

The Reds had closed their training camp in Mobile and were making their way north playing a series of games with minor league teams along the way. Marsans and Almeida boarded a train in Jacksonville and joined the Reds in Birmingham on the 20th. Tinker spoke to each of the Cubans individually, handling the situation with skill. He fined Marsans and Almeida $25 each for reporting late and warned the Cubans if they reported late in 1914 that they would be fined $100. Neither voiced any resentment toward their new manager. Marsans's play the next day soothed Tinker's frustration. He was three for four in the game against Birmingham, scoring one run and outhitting all of his Reds teammates.

While the Reds were in Birmingham, where Almeida had played for much of the 1912 season, his minor league manager spoke about the Cuban:

> He will never make a success as a big league player, because he takes too little interest in his work. When he came down here he was hitting .450 for a month or more, covering a world of ground and showing himself, apparently, the greatest ballplayer we ever saw in the South. Then he fell off, stopped exerting himself much on the field, and began to fan out on any kind of fast curve balls. He had walloped so hard at the start that he hit .301 for the season, but he wasn't doing anything the last six weeks or so. Great physical ability, but temperament isn't right for a ballplayer.[14]

In 1913, as a result of Marsans's performance the previous year there were six Cubans in spring training with major league clubs: Marsans and Almeida with Cincinnati; Jacinto del Calvo and Baldomero "Merito" Acosta with Washington; Miguel Angel González with Boston; and Alfredo Cabrera, Marsans's old teammate in New Britain, with the St. Louis Cardinals.

Clark Griffith, who had been manager of the Reds when Marsans broke into the National League, was managing the Washington team in 1913. He was responsible for signing Merito Acosta and Jacinto del Calvo. Acosta was just sixteen years old and was a sensation as an infielder. Del Calvo was also young, only eighteen at the time. A believer in the abilities of Cuban players since his experience with Marsans and Almeida in 1911, Griffith would develop the Senators into one of the major conduits for Latinos to enter the major leagues.

Miguel Angel González was a tall, gangly catcher, with ears sticking far out from his head. From behind the plate, González could snuff out an opponent's running game single-handedly. Base runners who would otherwise be stealing second and third were held back when the Cuban was behind the plate. He had joined the Boston Braves at the end of the 1912 and was returning for the 1913 season.

Alfredo Cabrera, who had played with the Indianapolis minor league team for the 1912 season, was finally given a chance in the major leagues. His skills as a shortstop were still revered. His unique ethnic background was also still in focus. "Cabrera is a

According to the *Cincinnati Tribune* (April 27, 1913), Marsans used a 35 ounce bat with a grip said to be no bigger than a broom handle, the narrowest in the league. (National Baseball Hall of Fame Library, Cooperstown, N.Y.)

dark man, very brown, but has the most Irish face you ever saw…. He is not a Spaniard, like Marsans, nor a Portuguese, like Almeida. This strange unit of a departed people is a guanche, or aborigine, of the Canary Islands."[15] The acceptance of Marsans and Almeida by America's baseball public had expanded the range of potential candidates for the major leagues, and Cabrera, who was probably too darkly complected to join Marsans and Almeida on the Reds in 1911, was now seen as being within that newly-expanded range.

Tinker's outfield was believed to be one of the best in baseball. Marsans, Bescher, and Bates were all exceptionally fast men. The trio would drive opponents crazy on the basepaths and it was going to be difficult to hit balls past them, even in Cincinnati's huge outfield.

Marsans was slated to play in right field. In Cincinnati, this was the sun field, meaning that the rightfielder at Redland Field faced directly into the sun in the early innings. He then dealt with the shadows falling across the field as the sun sank behind the grandstand. Marsans said,

> I have never played a sun field in Cuba where I have to face the sun as directly as I will have to do in Cincinnati, but I do not expect trouble…. A player who works in the sun field in Cincinnati has a hard time seeing the ball when he comes in from the field and has to bat right away. Most of the fellows who play that field have to let the first few balls pitched to them go by so they can get things gauged right. I may have to do that, but even if I do, I think I can hit up to my regular gait.[16]

Bad weather limited the 1913 opening day crowd in Cincinnati to 20,000. The Reds were outclassed by Pittsburgh and lost 9–2. Cincinnati sank into the second division and soon found themselves tied for last place with Boston with two wins and seven losses.

On Sunday, April 19th, the Reds were hosting the Chicago Cubs at Redland Field. The gong signaling the end of the Cubs batting practice had just rung and the Reds were taking the field for fielding practice. Marsans crossed the diamond, between third base and the pitcher's mound, heading to the outfield. Mike Mitchell, the former Reds captain who was traded to Chicago for Joe Tinker, hit one last batting-practice pitch. The ball shot off his bat and hit Marsans in the neck. The Cuban collapsed on the infield grass, unconscious. Players quickly formed a circle around him. Mitchell and the Reds' trainer carried him, still unconscious, off the field and into the clubhouse. Marsans's neck, just below the base of his skull, swelled dramatically. He regained consciousness after several minutes in considerable pain and with no idea what had occurred. The Reds' official doctor examined him, saying:

> Had the ball struck Marsans two inches higher the Reds would have had to get another right fielder. The ball would have fractured his skull, and as it came with terrific force, the blow would have been fatal.[17]

Marsans returned to the bench two days after the incident to loud applause from the Cincinnati fans. On April 23rd, a week after the accident, Marsans played for the first time after his injury. He earned a base on balls as a pinch-hitter in the ninth inning and scored a run. His head continued to bother him, but he wanted to return to his outfield position. In his first game back as an outfielder, he scored three runs and totaled four hits in nine plate appearances in the first two games. But he hit safely only once in the next four games. His average sank to .260. Tinker believed Marsans had not fully recovered, but he refused to stop playing.[18]

Being knocked unconcious by Mitchell's batting practice hit was the beginning of a season-long streak of injuries, both typical and aberrant, that cost Marsans thirty-five games in 1913.

Batting in a game in late April, Marsans moved around in the batter's box waiting for the pitch. The pitcher wound up and the ball zipped toward the plate. Soon after it left the pitcher's hand, Marsans realized the ball was going to arrive on the inside of the plate. He pulled back from the plate, but the ball hit the index finger of his right hand, smashing it against the bat. The umpire called it a foul ball, thinking the pitch had only hit the bat. Marsans showed him his injured finger and was granted first base for being hit by the pitch. Marsans was able to remain in the game, getting two singles. But in the last half of the fifth inning, the finger became too painful for him to continue. Marsans was back in the outfield for the game on the 3rd of May. His finger was still sore but that did not stop him from getting two hits and scoring two runs.

At the end of May, while Marsans was playing for the sick Dick Hoblitzell, a baserunner stepped on his foot as Marsans awaited the infielder's throw at first base. Players in 1913 wore leather shoes with chisel-like metal spikes affixed to the bottoms. Marsans hobbled to the players' bench and took off his shoe and sock. The trainer bound the wound with a bandage and Marsans returned to the game.

On the 30th of May, Marsans was spiked playing first base. Again, he had to go to the bench, where Joe Tinker bandaged the injury, but Marsans returned to his position amid cheers from the fans.[19]

After this string of injuries, Marsans began to hit his stride. His play was no longer marred by as many mental lapses as it had been in 1911 and 1912. Though he still missed the occasional flyball, it was clear that the sun in the difficult Cincinnati right field was often a factor. The only major flaw remaining in his game was his tendency to overslide bases. It is not clear what caused this. Was Marsans underestimating his own speed, or was his sliding technique faulty? On May 25th, in a typical incident, Marsans earned first base on a single and then took off for second, attempting to steal. He clearly beat the throw but slid past second base, allowing the Pittsburgh Pirates' second baseman to tag him out.[20]

Marsans was tied for the league lead in stolen bases by July's midpoint, with twenty-four steals in sixty-nine games. The Cuban stole seven more bases in the next twelve games to take sole possession of first place with .383 stolen bases per game. Marsans was now one of the best players on the Cincinnati Reds. Combined with his successes in 1912, his performance in the first half of the 1913 season assured him a place on the short list of the best baseball players in the world.

On June 10th in Philadelphia, Marsans and Almeida starred in front of a large Cuban contingent. Marsans made two exceptional catches from his position in right field, both with runners on base; one ball he caught barehanded while running at full speed toward the outfield fence. At the plate, Marsans drove in the tying run in the ninth inning. Almeida followed him at bat and drove Marsans home for the winning run.

Newspaper coverage of Marsans and Almeida had changed. The fictional sketches, first appearing in 1911, parodying the two Latinos' problems with English had disappeared. The following paragraph appeared in the May 25 *Cincinnati Tribune*: "Marsans created considerable amusement in the fifth inning of the second game when he dashed madly into the diamond after Huggins' pop. 'Geeve eet me,' shrieked the Cuban so that the entire West End could hear. Armando was accommodated and made a nice catch."[21] The reporting paints a believable image of a humorous incident that occurred as a result of Marsans's accent. This type of reporting neither portrayed the Cuban in a negative way nor denied that some of the events that happen to foreigners result from the differences in customs and language and are frequently humorous.

Marsans and Almeida had freed themselves from some of the stereotypes Americans held of Latinos. Their exposure to the fans of Cincinnati forced many to see the Cubans more as individuals instead of representatives of an ethnic group. But, as seen in the reports of a game in Brooklyn, stereotypes were still just below the surface. Marsans and Almeida shown brilliantly that day in front of a large contingent of their countrymen.

> The Latin temperament is truly a wonderful thing. After the great finish of the game which Marsans and Almeida won for the Reds by two timely hits, the delegation of Cubans rose up, overflowed, and surged to the dressing room. Dark little men with bristling mustaches seemed to rain into the place. They laughed, they sang; they shouted. They embraced Marsans and Almeida, and carried them on their shoulders. They wrung the hands of the other players, and one of them kissed Joe Tinker on the blushing cheek, where of Joe Tinker was moved to fervid oratory. For half an hour after the game the Cubans celebrated, and during the following evening a dozen banquets were held. Marsans and Almeida going from café to café in a taxicab and making a modest speech at every table.[22]

Almeida was at the center of trade rumors from the beginning of the 1913 season. He was seeing limited playing time as a result of the solid play of "Harvard" Eddie Grant at thirdbase. He was hailed for a ninth-inning, game-winning home run at the end of April, but when Tinker allowed Almeida to play third base for several games, the Cuban was erratic. He made exceptional defensive plays, but then over-threw first base or misplayed subsequent grounders. Though his hitting seemed to be improving in consistency, Almeida's base running lacked inspiration and polish.

Unable to displace the Reds' third baseman, Almeida pursued other options. He began to practice with the Reds' pitchers in the hope of finding a place on the pitching staff. Almeida also occasionally acted as the Reds' third base coach, where in one game he made the unusual move of throwing his arms around a base runner to stop him at third and prevent him from being thrown out at the plate. Tinker's plan was to develop Almeida into a utility infielder. He placed Almeida, who had become popular with Reds players, at shortstop when he himself could not play the position.[23] By May 11, Tinker had changed his mind and wrote to Herrmann saying he intended to make Almeida an outfielder. Tinker was trying hard to find Almeida a place because he batted so well against left-handed pitching.[24] In the end, however, Almeida's weaknesses outweighed his strengths, and the Reds sold him to Montreal of the International League. Almeida was to take the four o'clock train to Cincinnati to pack his trunk for Montreal. True to form, he missed the train and had to take the eight o'clock.

A subsequent article suggested that Almeida's departure was, at least partially, motivated by finances: "It looks as if a serious mistake was made in letting Almeida out in order to cut down expenses. A few games lost through not having enough utility players are more expensive than one man's salary."[25]

On July 19th, Marsans severely injured his ankle in a game in Philadelphia. After staying in bed for a day he went back to Cincinnati to recuperate while the team continued its road trip. After more than a week, the injury still had not healed. On July 28th, the doctors began to suspect that Marsans had injured ligaments in his ankle. He was still limping noticeably and could not run. Marsans was leading the league with thirty-one steals in sixty-one games before the injury but his lead eroded with each game missed. On July 31st, Marsans, still hampered by his ankle, appeared as a pinch hitter but flied out. A week later Marsans returned to the diamond and the crowd welcomed him back with a burst of applause. Marsans was limping slightly but he played through the pain and contributed significantly to the Reds' victory.[26]

On August 30th, Marsans came to the park with a high fever but told no one. Tinker, seeing how ill he looked, asked what was the matter and Marsans explained. The Cuban did not feel better the next day and stayed in his room during the game. Tinker sent Trainer Hoskins to see the Cuban, and Hoskins's reported to Tinker that Marsans no longer had a fever. Tinker gave Marsans a long talk on the trip to Pittsburgh the next day. At least one physician had advised Tinker that Marsans's persistent injuries were due to his year-round baseball schedule. He told Marsans he understood the Cuban was exhausted and ordered him not to play baseball in the winter in Cuba if he wanted to continue playing for the Reds. Tinker again showed aptitude in dealing with Marsans, though he did not believe he was up to the job of managing and admitted as much in a letter to Herrmann:

> I will confess that everything has been wrong this season. I have not shown you or the Cincinnati public anything in the way of being a manager. I am very sorry Mr. Herrmann, for all this, as I came to you and asked you to get me at a big cost and I have not made good. I don't believe I am a manager, but I can go out there and play shortstop for you and I believe could do more good for the team as a player than trying to play shortstop and manager at the same time.[27]

Marsans came back to the game with a vengeance, getting seven hits in his first nine at bats after his illness. As of September 7th, Marsans was fifth in the league in total bases stolen, with thirty-two. He stole two bases on September 10, the first since August 11. Future Hall of Famer Max "Scoops" Carey of Pittsurgh had taken a commanding lead during Marsans's absence with forty-nine stolen bases in 130 games.

Despite his injuries, Marsans, continued to interest other managers. John McGraw of the New York Giants made overtures to Tinker about a trade involving the Cuban. Clark Griffith of the Washington Senators, persistent in his attempts to again have Marsans on his team, wrote Herrmann in late September asking if he were interested in trading Marsans. The answer to both queries was no. Though his injuries had been a problem, Herrmann knew that Marsans was an integral part of the Reds and a great draw for the fans.

The Reds' season closed with Cincinnati in seventh place in the National League. Marsans remained with the team after the end of the season to play several games against minor league teams, and then returned to Cuba. Against Tinker's wishes, Marsans took his usual place with the Almendares team in Cuba for the winter season.

6

Conflict

The chain of events that culminated in the First World War was not far off as players and fans made ready for the 1914 base-ball season. Conflict also erupted in baseball that year. From humble beginnings as the Columbia League in 1913, a rival to organized baseball developed. The "outlaw" organization—called such because it did not operate under the aegis of the National Agreement—became the Federal League in 1914. It posed a serious threat to the monopoly that organized baseball held on the professional sport in North America.

The Federal League suffered financial problems until James A. Gilmore, a mid-western manufacturer and a veteran of the Spanish-American War, became the league's president in a well-orchestrated coup near the end of the 1913 season. Gilmore's friendly face gave little evidence of his competitive personality. He was an energetic, charismatic leader possessed of innate skills as a promoter. He soon recruited a group of wealthy men to back the new league. They were bakery magnates, restaurateurs, oilmen, and brewery owners. All shared a love for baseball and an unquestioned devotion to Gilmore. They would,

> render a conspicuous service to baseball, having seen what
> manner of men they are and the prospect they offer for a new

era in the game, if the public prefer the beer-guzzling, whiskey-befuddled magnate of the old-school, why, that is their own outlook.[1]

Gilmore promised that the league did not intend to challenge organized baseball, and that it wished to exist peacefully alongside the major and minor leagues. He gave assurances that the new league would not attempt to sign players committed to National Agreement teams, but would use only unsigned players.

The league's first major triumph was signing Joe Tinker to play for, and manage, the Chicago franchise. After the 1913 season Tinker was unsigned and feuding with August Herrmann. Though near the end of his career, Tinker was among the best known players of his day. His signing gave the new league credibility with fans and also with other players.

January 1914 was only fourteen days old when "Reindeer" Bill Killefer, a mediocre catcher for the Philadelphia Phillies, signed a Federal League contract. Philadelphia had not offered Killefer a contract for the 1914 season, and the Federal League took advantage. Soon after his signing with the Federal League, Philadelphia enticed Killefer to re-sign for the 1914 season. The Federal League sued the Philadelphia franchise. In the case, the judge ruled against the Federals for having signed Killefer who was under "moral if not legal" obligation to play with Philadelphia.[2] Killefer benefited financially from the existence of the new league, as would other players. His 1913 salary with Philadelphia was $3200. The Federal League signed him for $5800. Twelve days later he resigned with Philadelphia for $6500.[3]

Gilmore, in the wake of the decision, stated that if organized baseball would not respect Federal League contracts, the Federal League would not respect organized baseball's contracts. Gilmore gave the Federal League teams approval to try to sign any player they could. He planned to force organized baseball to the negotiating table by raising players' salaries dramatically in a bidding war. Gilmore was confident his financial backing would scare the other baseball magnates into a non-competition pact.

The Federal League's impact on organized baseball became clear when the new league announced its rosters in the spring. Fifty-nine players had jumped from major league teams to join the Federal League for the new season.[4] Before the Federal League's end, 172 players who had played in the National or American

Leagues would join the Federal League.[5] The majority of National or American League players who joined the Federal League were either marginal players with limited playing time in the big leagues or players at the end of their careers. To abandon organized baseball for the "outlaw" league was a bold move for a player. Despite the larger salary, a player was risking his career in such a move. If the Federal League collapsed, the player would be left without salary and, according to Rule 20 of the National Agreement, punished with a three-year suspension.

This did not prevent the Federal League from targeting the biggest stars in baseball. Ty Cobb met with Gilmore several times during 1914 and 1915, but never committed to play with the Federal League. Walter Johnson of the Washington Senators, one of the greatest pitchers of his era, did sign a contract with the Federal League at a salary of a phenomenal $17,000 per year for two years. Like Killefer, Johnson eventually rescinded his decision and rejoined the Senators.

Baseball historians dispute whether the Federal League was in fact a "major league." What can be said is that 172 of the 286 men who played in the Federal League had major league experience. Of the 114 players who had not played in the major leagues, twenty-five went on to play in the American or National League. Six men who played in the Federal League were later enshrined at Cooperstown: Albert "Chief" Bender, Mordecai "Three Finger" Brown, Bill McKechnie, Eddie Plank, Edd Roush, and Joe Tinker.

The promise of rain was palpable in the thick Kentucky air. Less than one hundred fans, scattered throughout the wooden grandstand of Louisville's Eclipse Park, watched the pre-season game. Each team pushed five players across home plate in the first nine innings. In the top of the tenth inning, Marsans stepped to the plate and dug into the batter's box. The count rose to two balls and two strikes. Marsans swung hard at the next pitch, bat and ball connecting with a loud crack. The line drive made the gap and rolled to the outfield fence as Marsans, already past first, headed for second. The ball bounced against the outfield wall and rolled slowly over the rough dirt of the warning track. Marsans glanced at the outfielder bending over to pick up the ball and, without hesitation, ran toward third, touching second base in stride. The throw to third was a good one. As the Cuban stretched his spiked feet toward the white canvas bag, the ball waited for him in the third baseman's glove. Marsans was out. The minor league Louisville Colonels then scored in their half of the inning to win the game.

Marsans sat on the bench the next day in pain, nursing his left shoulder, which had been hurt in his unsuccessful slide into third base the previous day. The Reds lost to Louisville again, 5–2. After the game, "Buck" Herzog, the Reds' new manager, unconvinced of the severity of Marsans's injury and frustrated by the failings of his new team, told the team physicians to examine his star left fielder. The two doctors concluded the injury was not serious and Herzog ordered Marsans to report in uniform, ready to play, the next day.

In pre-game warm-ups the subsequent day, Marsans ran over the cut grass of the Louisville outfield as fly balls ended their arcs in his glove. The team went through its pre-game ritual, players stretching, running sprints, and playing catch amid their own chatter and the repetitive cries of vendors in the stands. One by one the Reds took batting practice, hitting reduced-speed pitches around the field.

When Herzog told Marsans it was his turn to bat, Marsans reluctantly stepped to the plate. He scraped the dirt with his cleats and signaled for a pitch. Marsans grimaced in pain as he swung at the ball. He stood ready for the next pitch holding the bat with only his uninjured right arm. This perceived challenge to Herzog's authority incensed the new manager. He harshly questioned the veracity of Marsans's injury. Marsans did not tolerate his honor being impugned—he dropped his bat and walked off the field. Herzog yelled: "I suppose you know what it means for you if you leave this field without permission." Marsans continued walking and left the field without looking back. He borrowed a nickel from a bystander and rode the streetcar back to the hotel wearing his flannel uniform and black spikes.[6]

The Cuban was an enigma to Charles Lincoln "Buck" Herzog. Marsans's sophistication and accent were foreign to his new manager, but it was the way he played baseball that most perplexed Herzog. Each play seemed to be an expression of Marsans's love for the game and a celebration of the moment. Herzog was not endowed with Marsans's exceptional physical gifts. He was fast, but he did not possess the Cuban's extraordinarily swift legs to carry him from base to base or propel him over the wide, green expanse of the outfield with the speed that earned the respect of opponents and the adoration of the fans. He pursued baseball the way a dedicated middle-level factory manager approaches his work, as though some day the game itself would be obligated to reward his devotion by revealing its intricacies and secrets, and it had. A man such as Herzog could never understand that Marsans's commitment to baseball was one of passion, not pragmatism. Instead of viewing Marsans's accomplishments on the field, Herzog only saw what he thought was Marsans's wasted ability. In Herzog's view the Cuban's undeniable skills were being squandered through a lack of discipline and effort.

Buck Herzog, Marsans's manager and nemesis in Cincinnati. (National Baseball Hall of Fame Library, Cooperstown, N.Y.)

Though Marsans had reached elite status in professional baseball through hard work and dedication, in Herzog's eyes he was lazy and unfocused.

Herzog's face reminded people of a bird of prey. His prominent brow shadowed a large, beak-like nose. Though only twenty-eight years old, he had already played in and lost three World Series with John McGraw's New York Giants. Three times during Herzog's career, McGraw traded him, and twice the Giants reacquired him. McGraw was caught between his incompatibility with the headstrong player and the need for Herzog's deep understanding of the game. "I cannot stand having him on my ball club telling me what to do much of the time instead of taking orders from me," said McGraw, "but I need him on my club if I am to win pennants."[7]

Herzog was beginning his first season as the Cincinnati Reds player-manager, a role in which he would both anchor the Reds' infield at shortstop and make all managerial decisions. Herzog was one of four player-managers in the National League in 1914. The concept has since faded in popularity, with only a handful of men filling both roles in the post–World-War-II era, the last being Pete Rose, of the Cincinnati Reds, in 1986.

During the Reds' spring training, which had begun two months earlier in Alexandria, Louisiana, the team progressed substantially under Herzog's leadership. Despite bad weather and the occasional injury (including a wound inflicted by a turtle living in a fountain in the team's hotel), the team began to coalesce under Herzog. His managerial strategy was a mix of what he had learned from John McGraw and what he had gleaned from his experience as a player. To keep his opponents guessing, Herzog, in a tactic borrowed from McGraw, often had all of his pitchers warm up before a game and picked the one who was throwing best to start. Herzog also instructed the Reds in a new way to round first base in the event of an extra-base hit. He told his players to run directly to first, cut a sharp turn, and go directly on to second. Traditionally, players ran a large curve around first and approached second in an arc that connected the two bases. The tactic was christened "the tango dip," and the team immediately adopted the new approach.

Before the Marsans-Herzog conflict in Louisville, the Reds had stopped in New Orleans, where they won a hard-fought 3–1 game against the minor league Pelicans. Marsans was two for three with a sacrifice hit in the game. After succumbing to the Pelicans 4–2 the next day, the team headed for Memphis. There, they lost the first game against the minor league team 4–0. Major league teams from Chicago, New York, and Detroit had all beaten Memphis earlier that spring. Herzog said he had "never seen a club before that could see defeat coming with a smile, and go laughing and singing home to dinner after being shut out by a minor league club." In Herzog's opinion, the Reds long-standing tradition of mediocrity was responsible for their poor showing. Bluntly, he said, "loafing and stalling ... has been a characteristic of the Reds for many years."[8]

The train from Louisville arrived in Cincinnati at 9:45 PM, half an hour late, with the thrice-vanquished Reds on board. Marsans spoke to a reporter as he walked through the crowd and out of the station: "I am through with the Cincinnati baseball team for as long as Charles Herzog is manager of the team." He took a taxi to the once grand, Cincinnati landmark, the Burnet House Hotel, which served as a place of residence for many of the players during the season.

After going upstairs and putting his things in his room, he related the story of the incident with Herzog in Louisville to a *Cincinnati Enquirer* reporter: "During the first game at Louisville I hurt my left shoulder sliding to third base. It caused me great pain and did not seem to yield to treatment at all. This afternoon I went to the park at Louisville and when asked by [teammate] Rube Benton if I were going to play I said that I was not as my shoulder was paining me severely. I went to the outfield, however, for practice and chased flies for a time." When Herzog told him he was going to play that day, Marsans responded by saying he felt it was impossible due to his injury. "He spoke roughly to me and told me I would have to do it anyway," said Marsans. "Johnson was pitching to the batters and I tried one swipe at the ball, but the pain was so great that I involuntarily let go of the bat with one hand. Herzog again called me, saying that I was faking, that I was lying when I said my shoulder was sore ... I could not stand such treatment...."[9]

Herzog, indignant, declined to comment. Marsans had been the last player to report to spring training and did so only five days prior to the closing of camp. In Herzog's view, Marsans arrived out of shape and practiced with little effort or energy.[10] Marsans had wired August Herrmann, the Cincinnati Reds' president, that he could not report any sooner because his presence was required to manage Fabrica Tobacos de A. Marsans y Ca, his cigar factory in Cuba, while his father, and partner, was away in Mexico. Though he chose not to disseminate his view, Herzog believed the Cuban was placing himself above the importance of the team.

Marsans made an appointment to see August Herrmann the next day at his office. The contrast between the two men was dramatic. Marsans's athleticism was palpable in his appearance, while Herrmann was a corpulent lover of food and drink. The softness of Marsans's Cuban-accented English was the opposite of Herrmann's guttural, teutonic speech. Yet, the two men shared a passion for life and had grown fond of one another in Marsans's two and a half years with the Reds. Marsans explained what had happened in Louisville and reiterated his ultimatum; he would not play for the Reds if Herzog remained their manager.

Herrmann refused to act. He placed the responsibility of the day-to-day running of the Reds in his manager's hands. Marsans said to a reporter:

> I have been one of the few members of the Cincinnati team who have not been charged with loafing in the past three seasons. I always play to win. I do not play baseball solely for money as many other players, but because I love the game....
> Herzog has peculiar ideas about managing a ball club. He doesn't appreciate the differences in temperament among his men. He treats the conscientious, hard-working player in the same way that he does the loafer. He treats all like inferior beings; he never mingles with his men and only speaks to them to criticize them. To a man who is giving his best this lack of appreciation is disheartening and its accompanying injustice is such that I am through with the game if I have to play with such a man.[11]

Herzog stood his ground, stating that he did not know if Marsans would ever play for the Reds again and that he did not care.[12] The press supported his stand. The papers portrayed Marsans through existing stereotypes: "...it now seems that his jump was not the result of Federal [League] temptings, but due to his Latin temperament," wrote one reporter. "A Spaniard is a temperamental being. A call-down that only makes an American ballplayer chuckle is, to a Spaniard, deadly insult," wrote another reporter.

Two days later Marsans's conviction began to weaken. Several friends urged him to go to Herzog and apologize. At first, Marsans refused. Then he asked Herrmann to be his emissary. Herrmann declined.[13] The next day, Marsans capitulated. He went to Herzog and apologized for his departure from the field in Louisville. In their meeting, Herzog tried to impress upon the Cuban the need for discipline on the team. When Herzog told Marsans he would be fined $100 for leaving the field and staying away from practice for three days, Marsans balked. He walked out of the meeting and again threatened to quit, but he returned shortly and made peace with Herzog. But before returning, Marsans wanted to reinforce that Herzog's accusation of faking the injury was false and did so by telling reporters his shoulder was still sore but he would report to Redland Field the next day.

"Herzog and Marsans got the big hands when they came up to the plate for the first time, showing that everyone is pleased at the renewed pleasant relations between the manager and the crack outfielder."[14] In testament to the City of Cincinnati's devotion to its team, 15,728 fans gathered under steady rain to watch the Reds play the Chicago Cubs on opening day. They huddled under black umbrellas or sought shelter in the grandstand. The band played and the rain refused to stop as the players warmed up along the sidelines. A new white canvas tarp still covered the infield. In the pre-game conference of managers and umpires at home plate, Herzog's excitement convinced the others that the game should be played despite the weather.

Reds players Burke and Hoblitzell received loud applause for dancing an impromptu tango in front of their dugout wearing heavy-knit team cardigans over their flannel outfits. The 1914 Reds home uniforms were white, with red pinstripes, red trim around the collars, and the Reds logo on the left breast. The players wore loose, white, long-sleeved T-shirts that extended past the three-quarter length uniform sleeves. Their wool hats were short-billed with simple red C's on the front, closely resembling English schoolboys' caps. The baggy pants, cinched at the waist with black leather belts, ended tightly around the knees. Thick socks, red on the top and white from mid-calf down, covered their lower legs from knees to black, cleated shoes.

The Reds took the field to the sound of a standing ovation. The first Chicago Cub to bat hit a lazy fly and Marsans squeezed the ball in his glove as it fell out of the sky to record the first out of the 1914 season.

Marsans had become one of a handful of players in professional baseball who could dominate a game. He created runs with his stellar speed, which he used to score two runs on two walks and a single in four plate appearances on Opening Day. Rain continued to fall throughout the game, soaking players, fans and field. The Reds dominated the Cubs in a 10–1 victory.

As the fans filed out of Redland Field, some dreamed of a pennant but most were content to hope for a respectable season, something they had been denied for years; Cincinnati had not had a winning record since 1909 and had not finished above fourth in the National League in ten years.

It was not only the fans who felt the excitement in the potential of a new season. Herzog held practice the next day under the grandstand, the only bit of dry ground at Redland Field. The Reds had acquired Cuban Miguel Angel González. The tall, gangly catcher had been with Boston at the end of 1912 and the beginning of 1913 but was released due, in part, to his problems with English. He impressed Herzog that day by five times hitting a wooden peg two inches by five with a baseball from a distance equal to that of home plate to the pitcher's mound.

Veteran pitcher Red Ames told Herzog he could outdo the Cuban. He led his manager to a dark corner and placed a similar stake in the ground. Ames then paced off the distance from home plate to second base. He faced the peg, wound up and threw, sending the wooden piece flying. Herzog was incredulous but Ames did it again, then three times more without a miss. On the sixth try Ames threw far to the left of the peg but it still jumped in the air. Herzog walked to the peg and saw there was a string attached to it. He followed the string around a corner and found a giggling Earl Yingling, who had been tugging the string each time Ames threw.[15]

The war between organized baseball and the Federal League was escalating. The Reds suffered the loss of their Native American pitcher George "Chief" Johnson early in the season. The pitcher's signing with the Federal League was front-page news in Cincinnati on the 21st of April.

C.C. Madison, president of the Kansas City Federal League team, had contacted both Marsans and Johnson through an intermediary and invited them to his room in the Sinton, then the leading hotel in Cincinnati. Madison awaited the players in the luxurious suite. He invited Marsans in and made him an unknown

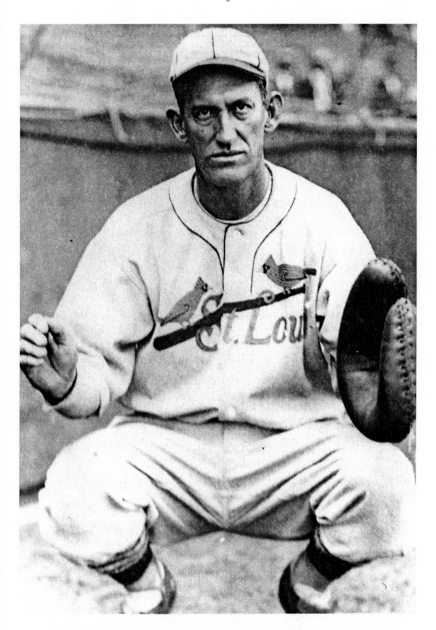

Miguel González, Marsan's teammate on the 1914 Cincinnati Reds. González would become the first Latino to manage in the major leagues, with the St. Louis Cardinals. (National Baseball Hall of Fame Library, Cooperstown, N.Y.)

offer to join the Federal League. The Cuban declined and left as
Johnson entered the room.

After niceties were exchanged, Madison escorted Johnson to
a restaurant on Vine St., the center of Cincinnati's boisterous
nightlife. After dinner, they returned to the Sinton. The baseball
man from Kansas City placed a valise on the table in the center
of the room. He reached into it and pulled out a stack of new $100
bills. Madison first offered Johnson a $2500 signing bonus to
become a Federal League player. Johnson considered for several
minutes then slowly shook his square-jawed head. Madison
counted out the signing bonus in twenty-five $100 dollar bills. He
paused to look at Johnson. Madison then counted out five more.
"How's that?" he asked, "and $5,000 a year for three years, the
contract to be signed tomorrow in St. Louis?"

A smile slowly emerged from Johnson's lips as his face lit up.
He took the bundle of money, wrote out a receipt and shook Madison's
hand. The former Red went back to the Burnet House,
packed his bags, and paid his bill. Johnson boarded the B&O at
9:20 that night, bound for Kansas City via St. Louis, where he
would sign his new contract.[16]

The facilitator of the deal was Joe Shreckel, recently fired
from his job as clubhouse boy by the Reds. Joe Tinker, the Reds'
manager during the 1913 season, promised Schreckel a job as
groundskeeper with his new team, the Chicago Federals, if he
could entice any of the Reds to join the new league. "The local
team turned me out to shift for myself after I asked for an increase
in salary this year," explained Shreckel, "and I am going to get
back at them to the best of my ability." He added ominously, as he
left for his new job in Chicago, that the Federal representatives
would try to induce pitcher Rube Benton and one other Red to
join them when the Cincinnati club was in Chicago the following
week.[17]

The directors of the Cincinnati Amusement Company, the
organization that owned the Reds, called an emergency meeting
to formulate a strategy to counter the Federal League's raid. The
Reds enacted their strategy on the 22nd of April, when "Chief"
Johnson, pitching in his first game as a Kansas City Packer in
Chicago, was served with a legal injunction while on the mound.
The temporary injunction prohibited him from playing for any
team but the Cincinnati Reds and also allowed him a semi-honorable
departure from an embarrassing pitching performance that

the Packers lost 9–1. The injunction required Johnson to cease performing as a baseball player until his case could be settled in a court of law.

The "Chief" Johnson case was one of the first major battles in the Federal League–organized baseball war. The opposing leagues poured their resources and their best legal minds into the action. If the Federal League's raiding tactics were upheld as legal, their strong financial backing would allow them to lure away many of the most popular players in organized baseball. With these players they could attract a baseball public that was still open to the idea of a third league.

As promised by Joe Shreckel, the Federal League again targeted the Reds. C.C. Madison approached Marsans and Rube Benton in the lobby of Chicago's LaSalle Hotel. Marsans declined to speak with Madison. Benton shook his head in solidarity with his teammate and the encounter was over.[18] August Herrmann was outraged. "We will not stand for honest players like Marsans and Benton being constantly tempted by these outlaws…. Such action is contrary to all law and justice, and will not be upheld in the court or in the minds of fair-minded people."[19]

In an organizational oversight, the Reds stayed in the same hotel in St. Louis as the Pittsburgh Federals in early May. This allowed players to compare the virtues of the leagues.[20] Seven Cincinnati Reds listened to Federal League offers and decided to change leagues if the ruling went in favor of Johnson.[21] "Rebel" Oakes, manager of the Pittsburgh Federal League Club, and Mordecai Brown, the St. Louis Federals manager, negotiated the deal with Reds players Rube Benton and Tom Clarke, who acted as agents for the other five undisclosed Reds.

On June 3rd, the judge in Superior Court of Cook County ruled to uphold the injunction, which prohibited Johnson from playing for any team other than the Reds. Johnson responded, "All the decisions or injunctions in the world can't make me go back to Cincinnati."[22]

The Federal League attempted to circumvent the ruling by having Johnson play in every city outside of Cook County, where the injunction was issued. August Herrmann quickly countered this stratagem, promising to file injunctions in all of the Federal League cities. Herrmann was less concerned with the future of his pitcher than with the triumph over the Federal League. He called the ruling "a great victory for baseball" and something that "saves and preserves, as well, the honor and integrity of the game and its players."[23]

The day the Johnson case was decided, two identically phrased letters arrived on Herrmann's desk. One was from young Reds pitcher Dave Davenport, the other from Armando Marsans. Marsans acknowledged he had received legal counsel from a Federal League representative while he was in St. Louis. The lawyer advised Marsans and Davenport how to phrase the letters to Herrmann. The letters declared the players' current contracts null and void based on their lack of mutuality, particularly with regard to Clause Seven of the standard player contract with organized baseball, known as the "Ten-day Clause." The clause read:

> The club may, at any time, after beginning and prior to the completion of the period of this contract, give the player ten days' written notice to end and determine all its liabilities and obligations hereunder, in which event the liabilities and obligations undertaken by the club shall cease and determine at the expiration of said ten days. The player, at expiration of said ten days, shall be freed and discharged from all obligation to render service to the club. If such notice be given to the player while "abroad" with the club he shall be entitled to his traveling expenses, including Pullman accommodations and meals en route.

This clause, in effect, gave clubs the power to fire players with only ten days' notice.

The players contended the Ten-day Clause, which allowed teams to release players without explanation, was not reciprocal. Asserting their right to mutuality, the letters from Marsans and Davenport closed: "You must within two days of the receipt of this notice offer me terms satisfactory to me or I will after two days consider myself free of contract to render my services elsewhere after expiration of said ten days."

Clause Ten, known as the Reserve Clause, also favored the owners. Thus, clubs could resign players from year to year at the same salary. It read:

> The player will, at the option of the club, enter into a contract for the succeeding season upon all the terms and conditions of this contract ... and the salary to be paid the player in the event of such renewal shall be the same as the total compensation

provided for the payer in Clause One hereof, unless it be
increased or decreased by mutual agreement.

Herrmann forwarded Marsans's and Davenport's letters to
Herzog. When the two players arrived on the field for practice
before the day's game, Herzog notified them they were suspended.
He told them to get off the field and turn in their uniforms.[24] The
player-manager told reporters,

> Marsans is the disturber. He resents my efforts to make him
> play ball hard for the good of the club and will not take the
> criticism that is coming to every player now and then.... I have
> known for some time that Marsans was sulking and trying to
> stir up trouble among the other players. He has been to see me
> twice to have his salary raised, though he willingly signed a
> three-year contract at a liberal figure only a short time ago. I
> could not see any reason for granting his request, as he has
> been out of the game more than any other regular, and is so
> easily hurt that he is liable to be out of any important series.[25]

Marsans, the player who earned praise for his work ethic and
devotion to the team during the 1912 and 1913 season, was again
being painted by Herzog as an inherently lazy malcontent. With
each day that Marsans performed so well for the Reds in those previous seasons, he showed the people of Cincinnati and the United
States that he was an individual, as were all Latinos. As Cincinnati
got to know him, he challenged stereotypes through this individ-
uality. But, as soon as there was unrest, the pejorative stereotypes
emerged to explain his actions.

Did Marsans exert himself less as his stardom grew? There is
no evidence to support this. It is true that a series of injuries and
illnesses had plagued Marsans during Herzog's short tenure. After
the shoulder injury, a cold had confined the Cuban to his room
for several days. The number of games Marsans missed increased
each year he played for the Reds, most likely due to a grueling
year-round schedule of baseball in the U.S. and Cuba. Despite his
absences, Marsans continued to be one of Cincinnati's best players, and among the top players in the National League. At the
time of his suspension, he was second in the league with thirteen
stolen bases and was batting .298.[26]

Herzog's personal confrontation with Marsans had come to
a head for a second time only five days earlier. The Sunday sun

shone down on a near-record crowd of 26,000 at Redland Field. Men in starched white shirts with celluloid collars sat on the field in foul territory watching the game, their jackets on their laps, and straw boaters on their heads. Special ground rules had to be adopted to cope with the overcrowding. The managers agreed with the umpires in their pre-game meeting that only two bases— a ground rule double—would be given for fair balls that found their way into the crowds on field level.

In the sixth inning of the first game of the doubleheader, Marsans was on first. The Pirates' 190 pound, six-footer, "Hickory" Bob Harmon was on the mound. The score was 1–0 in favor of the Reds. As Harmon began his windup, Marsans turned and took several rapid, choppy steps toward second. His stride lengthened as he reached full speed. Marsans thrust his feet in front of him as he slid, the base easily stolen. But he had miscalculated. He began his slide too late, his momentum carrying him almost past second base. Honus Wagner, the wily Pirates shortstop and future Hall of Famer, took advantage of Marsans's mistake. With a nudge unseen by the umpire, Wagner pushed Marsans off the bag. He then tagged the Cuban out. Standing on top of the base, the Cuban vehemently argued his case but the umpire refused to yield. The umpire ejected Marsans when he persisted in his disagreement.[27]

Herzog, while not disputing that Marsans had received a bad call, saw the ejection as the result of Marsans's unchecked ego; the ejection was a result of selfishness that hurt the team at a crucial moment by depriving it of its best player. Herzog roughly criticized Marsans who stared his manager in the eye but said nothing and took his place on the bench, the team enveloped in silence. Herzog later described Marsans's behavior in the following way:

> While I knew that Marsans had been handed a rough deal by the umpire, we needed every particle of strength so much that any valuable man getting himself put out of a game hurts us heavily. When I told him so he sulked, and for the twentieth time, showed that his individual glory was more to him than the success or united playing system of the team. The Cuban is a great ballplayer... I can hardly say how great a star he is lest I should seem extravagant in my praise. Yet while he thinks of his own playing more than the prospects of the club, he can hardly be called a winning player.[28]

The Cuban newspaper *La Prensa* pointed out that there was a lack of understanding, cultural as much as personal, in Herzog's interpretation of Marsans's action. "Herzog, far from saying Marsans was in the right and understanding that the Cuban was trying to win and defend his rights, the rights of his club, criticized him violently, saying things that Armando did not need to tolerate...."[29]

The *Cincinnati Times-Star* was also laudably even-handed:

> When Marsans was thrown out of the game May 31, he thought, from his point of view, that he had fought and suffered for the club, and that Herzog should applaud him. When he received a sharp call and was informed that he had shown himself a bonehead by his fiery attack on the umpire, he went up in the air and thinking himself hurt, slighted, abused, went away in savage anger. Marsans never realized that it was his extreme value to the team that provoked his scolding. Herzog, needing every high-class man, was rightfully offended when such a man got himself thrown out of the game, crippling the team. Any manager would have called Marsans down. Thinking of all these things, what is to prevent, in all fairness and justice to all concerned, the pardon of Marsans?[30]

Herzog was not in the mood to pardon Marsans; it had become a contest of wills. Herrmann officially notified Marsans and Davenport of their suspensions in writing before the game that afternoon, stipulating that Marsans would only be reinstated after he made a public apology. Herzog added his own criterion, "Until he comes to his senses and shows a disposition to play ball as well as he can he will remain under suspension."[31] Marsans and Davenport watched the game from the stands, and afterwards Marsans asked Herrmann for a day to contemplate his options. The team president granted Marsans his wish. Though he was lenient with Marsans privately, publicly Herrmann was resolute:

> We will have discipline at any cost. Contracts must be respected on all sides and disturbers will be dealt with harshly no matter how their loss will hurt the team in a temporary sense. The men who have complained are receiving generous salaries, and only a few days ago expressed themselves as highly content with their lot.[32]

In fact, as Herzog had revealed on May 31, Marsans had repeatedly expressed discontent with his salary. And just the previous day, explaining his position to reporters, Marsans had said:

> My complaint is this: Several players on the club, Yingling, Benton and Douglas, have been given new contracts that call for more money than they signed for at the beginning of the season and that do not contain the 10-day notice of release clause. I claim I am as good a ballplayer as they are, so why can't I get a raise in salary and a contract with the 10-day clause marked out?[33]

Marsans's dissatisfaction had been brewing since his arrival at spring training. Marsans had signed a three-year contract for $4,400 per year that winter, when Reds business manager Frank Bancroft visited him in Cuba for that purpose.[34] At that time there was only limited coverage in Cuban newspapers of the bidding war erupting between the Federal League and organized baseball. Only later, probably upon his arrival at spring training, did Marsans learn how other players' salaries had increased. Marsans was a wealthy man. The money was not the significant issue; how his salary compared to others is what vexed the Cuban. Marsans was, even by Herzog's admission, one of the ten best players in major league baseball, yet his salary was not commensurate with his ability and performance.

Herzog's two refusals to discuss a raise apparently were insults that increased the ill will that finally exploded with Marsans's ultimatum.

Marsans explained the sequence of events as follows:

> When I reported at the training camp and discovered the real reason for Bancroft's visit was the Federal League situation and that several of the Cincinnati players had received new contracts calling for a "substantial increase in salary," I went to Herzog and demanded a new contract. Herzog tried to bully me into believing that I could not jump to the Feds and when we made our first trip to St. Louis on May 6, I called on the St. Louis Federal League Club officials. I was willing to jump at that time but they did not want me to hurdle until certain court proceedings were settled. When the Johnson case was decided at Chicago last week they instructed me to serve the Cincinnati club with a ten-day notice of my intention to resign. When I informed Herzog that I intended to quit the club in

ten days unless tendered a new contract, he swore at me in an insulting manner and suspended me from duty with the threat that he would see to it that I was prohibited from playing with any team.

On the evening of June 3rd, the day of the suspensions, Davenport left for Boston with the other Reds. That afternoon he had apologized to Herzog and was reinstated to the team. Marsans made no apologies and remained in Cincinnati. Some of his teammates were angry that he was abandoning the team when they were winning and it seemed as if the pennant were a possibility. But at least seven of Marsans's teammates had reportedly planned to do the same when they thought the Johnson ruling would be in the Federal League's favor.

A pack of reporters mobbed Herzog when the Reds' train arrived at Boston's South Station. Herzog responded to their questions about the Marsans situation with the following statement:

> Marsans is under indefinite suspension and will remain so until I see fit to remove the ban. He has been a disturbing element all year and I will have discipline on this club if I have to sign up all semi-pros and bushers. Luckily the big majority of boys are the most earnest and conscientious workers a manager could desire, so outside of the Marsans fracas there has been little or no friction. I received word en route from Cincinnati that Marsans was willing to join the team when I send for him. When I will decide this, if ever, is problematical. We have a couple of very high-class outfielders and can get along without the Cuban if needs be. I may send for him tomorrow and may allow him to rusticate a week. It all depends on how he feels about the matter and whether he can show me once that he means to give me and the team his best services.[35]

In a moment of indecision, Marsans had sent a message to Herzog, saying he was willing to rejoin the team. Since a response was not forthcoming, Marsans decided he would board a train for Boston without word from Herzog, but an unidentified "legal friend" counseled him to wait in Cincinnati for a response.[36]

Marsans arranged an appointment with August Herrmann for June 4th. Herrmann, not one to be late for a meal, had already left for lunch at his social club when his star player arrived at his office. They spoke later by telephone. Marsans, probably intimidated by the uncertainty of joining the Federal League, said he was willing to rejoin the Reds with no raise, but Hermann said that reinstatement was up to Herzog, who still had not responded to Marsans. The Cuban's defiance then solidified. He said he would not rejoin the team but would stay in Cincinnati for a week reporting to the Reds' office every day.

The Cincinnati papers were divided between Marsans and Herzog. The *Enquirer* bemoaned the loss of Marsans: "This fellow is really so great a ball player, in so many ways, that his absence makes a hole you could drive a small mule through…. Balls have gone to the fence that he would have choked, and the need of his crashing hits and swift steals is felt each day." The same article praised Herzog, saying, "His quick action in the Marsans case stamps him as a leader of courage and ability far above the ordinary."[37]

The *Cincinnati Times-Star* said:

> Although the fans applaud the firm attitude of Manager Herzog in the Marsans case, yet the absence of Marsans is deplored. To say that his one-man rebellion is not injuring the team would be sheer nonsense. The bald fact remains that since Armando severed his connection with the team in temperamental style, the Reds have been thrown off their previous stride. Miller cannot begin to fill the spiked shoes of the capable Cuban in the left garden…. Right now, if the fans could vote on the question the majority for his retention at whatever sacrifice would be overwhelming.[38]

Herzog summed up his position with another statement to the press:

> What a ball player I'd have made out of this Marsans if he had only stuck to the colors! Mind you, when I speak of teaching Marsans, I am not conceited enough to talk of educating him in things where he was already my superior. Marsans could teach me things in batting, straightaway running, trapping fly balls—there was nothing I could show him mechanically, except, perhaps, how not to overslide a base—one fault he had at times. I'd have been glad to receive lessons from the Cuban in many things, and would have insisted that he teach me, too. Where I could have educated Marsans would have been in the points of team play—of making every effort count—of playing more for the club, less for his own glory. And he'd have become a wonder in a little while. I am sore at him for his behavior and I consider him a disorganizer. And yet I must admit that the Spaniard is a great ball player. He is too sensitive.

He should remember that baseball is a red-blooded game for rough and hardy men, and that the language that flies back and forth when such men are criticizing each other is often full of sulphur. He quits on the least bruise, quits if his temper is offended. Temperament, that's all—but what can a fellow do about it?[39]

Public sympathy for Marsans was overridden by anger about the timing of his actions. The Reds were in second place with a 26–17 record behind the 23–13 New York Giants. The majority of fans' opinions printed in an article in the *Cincinnati Post* were against Marsans. Tom Regan, a saloonist, said, "I don't think Marsans acted squarely. When he signed the contract, he knew what he was doing. If he wasn't satisfied, he should have objected." Doctor Gus Hickman said, "If the Cuban is dissatisfied, box him up and send him back to Cuba. He can do no good if he does not want to play with the Reds." The only support Marsans received in the article was from Joe Dixon, president of the city baseball league. Dixon said, "Marsans is a business man, and I believe he acted right. He was dissatisfied here, and when a man is dissatisfied with his job the best thing he can do is make a change."[40]

Herrmann publicly supported Herzog, but behind the scene he was preparing for every possibility. He was aware of Marsans's value as a player and in gate receipts, and enlisted the help of several friends in getting Marsans to rejoin the Reds. One of the agents described the pursuit:

Of all the tough jobs I ever tackled that man Marsans is certainly the worst ... I appealed to him in every possible manner, for your sake; for the sake of our team; for the sake of the baseball public who were so fond of him, but I could positively not budge him from his determination, viz.: that he would only report upon written orders from either you or Herzog ... judging from his conversation, he has received advice not to report unless upon written orders as above stated, for the reason that if he does and should go to Boston, as you suggest, he will jeopardize his rights in the matter (whatever that may be).... I am also of the opinion that his attorney has filled him full of visions of the recovery of a large sum of money from the Club through a suit for damages based on the fact, as he claims, that he was suspended without cause.... He must have also been advised to remain here ten days and to report each day at the

office and Redland Field—I guess that is some legal arrangement of his counsel. He also told me that a representative of
the Federal League team approached him last evening with a
$7000 cash bonus proposition.... He merely mentioned this as
an evidence that he has been approached, but assured me that
he had no intention of jumping....[41]

Though Marsans had announced that he would remain in
Cincinnati and report to the Reds office each day until his ten-day
notice expired, he left Cincinnati on short notice on the evening
of Friday, June 5th. His hasty departure for St. Louis was apparently prompted by a telegram he received that day from either his
lawyer in St. Louis or the Federal League officials. Marsans wired
his boarding house, into which he had moved at the beginning of
the season, to hold his room because he would be back within a
few days.[42]

Another of Herrmann's agents wrote the Reds' president to
propose a solution to the Marsans problem:

I spent the past winter in Cuba and I was with Mr. Marsans a
great deal and I think I know him fairly well. He is an obstinate
chap and very contrary, or in other words "you can't tell him
anything." Of course you know this, but you do not know that
there is really only one man who is his master, and who can
reason and talk to him and that man is his father.
I would suggest then Mr. Herrmann, that you cable his father
the circumstances and have the elder Marsans cable his son at
your expense. The results undoubtedly will be satisfactory to all
concerned, and the matter will be settled, within a day or two.
Mr. Herzog, with all his authority and the Board of Directors
with all their power and capital, cannot change Armando's
mind but temporarily. He is of course playing a baby act and I
am quite qure [sic] that his father can whip him and bring him
to time.... Another suggestion is that you get in touch with Mr.
Henry Straus, with whom Armando signed a contract to handle
his cigars in Cincinnati. Marsans is very enthusiastic about his
cigar business, and holds it closest to his heart. If he can be
made to realize that his actions with the Cincinnati Baseball
Club will not help the sale of his cigars, I am sure that he will
act differently.[43]

Crucial to the understanding of how Marsans was viewed by
the United States public was the perception of temperment. In 1911
sociologist Franz Boas had written:

> It is an impression obtained by many travelers, and also based upon experiences gained in our own country, that primitive man of all races, and the less educated of our own race, have in common a lack of control of emotions, that they give way more readily to an impulse than civilized man and the highly educated. This impression is based largely on the neglect to consider the occasions on which various forms of society demand a strong control of impulse.
>
> Most of the proofs of this alleged peculiarity are based on the fickleness and uncertainty of the disposition of primitive man, and on the strength of his passions aroused by seemingly trifling causes. Too often the traveler or student measures fickleness by the importance he himself attributes to the actions or the purposes in which they do not persevere, and he weighs the impulses for outburst of passion by his own standard.[44]

Because a predominant view held that these outbursts were manifestations of primitive character, Boas looked to primitive cultures to debunk the myth. He pointed to the fact primitive cultures practiced inhibition of impulses in the social customs and taboos of their culture. These inhibitions may not have coincided with the Edwardian customs practiced by many in the United States in Marsans's era, but they demonstrated clearly that members of primitive societies could inhibit their impulses as well as other peoples.[45]

Another prevailing belief about racial differences was that the development of the mental activities in civilized people from youth to adulthood accurately reflected the development of the human mind from primitive to civilized man. In other words, because Marsans's inability to inhibit his outbursts was seen as childish by Americans, it demonstrated that Marsans, typical of other Latinos, was a member of a race still in a state of development and, therefore, inferior to the highly advanced whites.[46]

Marsans's disagreement with the Reds prompted Archdeacon Dodson of the Grace Episcopal Church in Lebanon, Ohio, to deliver a sermon entitled "The Game of Life." Dodson compared the Federal League's offers to players in organized baseball to the Devil's temptations and urged the good people of his flock to stay in the "good league" and to make the "sacrifice hit" which would help their fellow man get to "home plate," but that their sins would make it a close call and "many will have to slide."[47]

Marsans arrived at St. Louis' huge fortress-like train station, on the morning of June 6th. Its single, brown limestone tower stood six stories tall and peered over the city like a sentinel.

Marsans walked outside the station and took a taxi to the American Hotel. Through Dwight Currie, his lawyer there, Marsans announced he was in St. Louis for an indefinite stay.[48] That same day he met with the owners of the St. Louis Terriers: Colonel Otto Stiefel, Philip Ball, Walter Fritsch, and President Edward A. Steininger. It is probable that in this noon meeting with the Federal League representatives, Marsans agreed to terms for a contract to play with the Terriers, but his legal position made it unwise for him to actually sign a contract until the ten-day notice he had served to the Reds had expired.

The Federal League had learned their lesson from the George "Chief" Johnson court case. Johnson, the former Reds pitcher, had signed with the Kansas City Federal League team within ten days of terminating his contract with the Reds. This discredited the Federal League's attempt to establish mutuality in a player's right to serve a ten-day notice to his club. With Marsans, they were careful not to make the same mistake.

Though he had yet to sign with the Federal League, Marsans made it clear that he was leaving the Reds for good. After the meeting, he cabled his boarding house at Garfield Place in Cincinnati asking for his belongings to be sent to him at the American Hotel. He also asked the Reds' groundskeeper to send his cleats and sliding pads to him in St. Louis.[49] As Marsans drifted farther away from organized baseball, he made sure not compromise his negotiations with the St. Louis Terriers. "I consulted with the Federal League men all day Saturday," he said, " but I have not signed, and do not propose to sign, until I have been guaranteed my terms. I have plenty of time; Why should I act in a hurry? If I do not play with the Federal League I will go back to Cuba and quit baseball for good."[50]

On Monday, June 8th, Otto Stiefel said he would make an announcement regarding Marsans's status on Friday, the day Marsans's ten-day notice to the Cincinnati Reds terminated.[51] While the Terriers waited for the days to elapse, they continued to court Marsans, taking him to the finest homes and restaurants in St. Louis and driving him through the city in opulent cars.[52] Throughout his tumultuous spring of 1914 with the Reds, Marsans's actions showed his feeling of under-appreciation. The treatment the St. Louis franchise gave him, in contrast, must have been especially attractive.

Organized baseball had sanctimoniously denounced the Federal League's method of luring players away from their contracts, but they soon adopted the same tactics, trying to bring back players who had signed Federal League contracts. Marsans was a tempting target. The St. Louis Browns of the American League offered him $500 to delay his signing with the Terriers, hoping they could negotiate a trade with the Reds.[53] He also received an offer from Clark Griffith to sign with the Washington Senators. At least six people visited Marsans in his room at the American Hotel, trying to get him to rejoin organized baseball. As a countermeasure, the Terriers moved him to the house of an undisclosed franchise shareholder, and assigned him an escort to prevent further approaches.

August Herrmann attempted to orchestrate a trade sending Marsans to the Chicago Cubs. If he were going to lose Marsans, he preferred to receive players in exchange instead of losing the Cuban to the Federal League without compensation. Herrmann wired Marsans with a proposal.[54] C.H. Thomas, the Chicago Cubs owner, sent no fewer than five telegrams.[55] Marsans ignored them all. The deal fell apart in the face of Marsans's resistance and the legal uncertainty of his eligibility to play for the Cubs.

Herrmann was calling upon anyone he could think of to help. Ben A. Hirschler, who had previously suggested that the best way to influence the Cuban was through his father, wrote to Marsans on June 11th:

> Mr. Armando Marsans
> American Hotel
> St. Louis, Mo.
> On behalf of Cincinnati fans, I hope you will show true Spanish chivalry and return to the Cincinnati Base-Ball Club. Cincinnati wants you—the Cincinnati Club needs you—Henry Straus needs you to help sell Fabrica Tobacos de A. Marsans y Ca.
> If you do not return to Cincinnati, the name of Marsans will suffer. You will not sell any cigars—you will have no friend in organized Base-Ball. Organized Base-Ball will not visit Cuba and Cuba will have lost some of its prestige in base-ball.
> By all means show true sportsmanship. Come back to Cincinnati and organized ball. It will mean much to you in your future business. Wire me collect.
> > Kindest regards from your friend
> > Ben A. Hirschler[56]

It is impossible to know Marsans's reaction to this letter. Its paternalistic tone may have exacerbated his feelings of mistreatment and lack of respect from the Reds.

The letter's threat that organized baseball would boycott Cuba was real. Any team or player that played against Marsans's Almendares team with Marsans on the field, while under suspension, would be in violation of the National Agreement and subject to punishment. The prospect is likely to have bothered Marsans, and he took advantage of the presence of Clark Griffith in St. Louis in early June to seek his advice. Griffith had been Marsans's manager with the Reds in 1911 and Marsans respected his judgment, spending over two hours in conference with him. Griffith summed up the meeting by saying:

> I told Marsans, simply, and with the sincerity and confidence that I use with him, not to pay attention to the Federal offers. I told him not to forget that he had made a name for himself and become famous in the National League, and had been treated well by the Cincinnati Club, that he had distinguished himself very much, and that he should remain loyal to Mr. Herrmann. I spoke with him a great deal, and gave him practical advice of common sense, and he listened to me, and promised he would weigh my advice and keep it in mind when he decided what to do.
> Marsans resents things easily and he explained to me that he could not get along with Herzog, whom I also know, and know that he has a bad temper. I know the Cuban well, he has to be managed in a certain way, treat him (jocularly), I never had any great trouble with him, and I have done everything I could to get him to go back to Herzog's team.[57]

Marsans's conference with Griffith demonstrates that the Cuban's inability to work with Herzog was not simply a problem with authority. Marsans demanded respect, and Griffith understood this. Herzog, with his tendency to treat Marsans like a self-centered, recalcitrant child, did not.

The Reds sent one last envoy to Marsans. He delivered by hand a telegram from Herzog to Herrmann that lifted Marsans's suspension.[58] Without agreeing to Marsans's demands, Herzog ordered him to join the Reds in Philadelphia on June 11th.[59] Marsans ignored the telegram, which was clearly intended to lay the groundwork for an imminent legal battle.

After it was announced that Marsans would play his first game for the Terriers on Sunday, June 14th, the Cuban returned to the American Hotel. The Federal League officials still feared organized baseball's agents enough that they stationed a guard outside Marsans's room every night to prevent him from being tempted away from the Federal League.[60]

7

No-Man's Land

The St. Louis Terriers needed Marsans's considerable talents. When Marsans first put on a Terriers uniform, the team was tied for last place in the eight-team Federal League with a record of 24–28. Despite that, they were only five and a half games out of first place. Handlan's Park, the Terriers' home at Grand and LaClede, seated about 25,000. The steel and concrete park, constructed by the Federal League franchise, cost $325,000. It measured 375 feet from home plate to the fence in center field, 325 to left, and a short 300 feet to right. The single level pavilion sloped up from the field at a low angle. It was covered with a roof supported by large I-beams rising out of the pavilion, which forced many spectators to crane their necks in order to watch the game.

Mordecai "Three Finger" Brown was the Terriers' manager (his moniker referred to a hand mutilated in a farming accident). Brown, Marsans's teammate with the Reds in 1913, was known as one of the true gentlemen in the game; when the Reds acquired him, the Hall of Fame pitcher advised them not to pay too much for him because he had injured his knee.[1] Other 1913 Reds players on the St. Louis Terriers were Ernie Herbert and Harry Chapman. In all, the 1914 Terriers had 17 players on their roster with major league experience.

103

In a tribute to Marsans's versatility, he batted clean-up and played shortstop in his first game as a Terrier. He would soon be moved to his usual outfield position, but for now he filled in for the Terriers' injured captain and regular shortstop, Al Bridwell. The Federal League officials chose a Sunday game, when the courts were closed, for Marsans's debut. They did not want the impact of the event to be undermined by Marsans receiving an injunction on the field.[2] Marsans committed two errors at the new position but "left no doubt in the minds of those that saw him perform, as to his ability as an infielder."[3]

At a few seconds past midnight, early Monday morning, June 15th, Armando Marsans signed a contract with the St. Louis Terriers that paid him $21,000 for three years. It was an increase of over 60 percent from his salary as a Red. Marsans wired Matty Schwab, the Reds' groundskeeper, requesting him to forward the rest of his equipment remaining in Cincinnati.[4] Marsans had crossed the Rubicon.

"Herrmann begged me to come back," the former Red told the press, "I told him my ultimatum was final. When I served my ten-day notice I informed him that I wanted a new contract, and with the reserve clause and ten-day release notice eliminated. He offered me a salary increase, but wanted me to waive all demands and rejoin the Reds, promising to see that I got a raise in salary. But he wanted to draw up the contract himself. That's where the hitch came in." Marsans took one last opportunity to establish culpability: "Herzog treated me very badly. I consider it only right that I receive a contract without the ten-day clause, and I gave the officials plenty of time to consider the matter."[5]

That same day, David Davenport joined Marsans at the American Hotel.[6] Davenport had demanded a new contract along with Marsans, but later begged for forgiveness. Herzog had taken him back on the team, blaming Marsans for corrupting the young pitcher. While the Reds were in Philadelphia, the pitcher asked Herzog for a fifteen-dollar advance and permission to stay in Philadelphia to visit a friend while the team traveled to Baltimore. Herzog agreed to both requests. That night, Davenport boarded the train for St. Louis. The lure of a substantially more generous contract, and perhaps residual friction with Herzog or his teammates led Davenport to St. Louis. He signed a three-year deal with the Terriers the next day and appeared in uniform at Handlan's Park that afternoon.[7]

Marsans played as the Terriers' second baseman in his second game. He flawlessly accepted seven fielding chances, had five hits in seven plate appearances, and scored the winning run in the twelfth inning.[8] The press raved, "His worth with the club cannot be estimated."[9]

While in St. Louis, Marsans continued to open doors for other Cuban baseball players. Manuel Cueto, a young Cuban third baseman, had begun the season with the Jacksonville team of the South Atlantic League but left the team after a dispute and was now playing in the independent Cigar City League in Tampa.[10] Marsans had been in contact with him since arriving in St. Louis and recommended him to the Terriers. The Terriers wired Cueto on the 22nd to come to St. Louis and paid for his transportation. Cueto arrived in St. Louis at noon on Thursday, June 24, hurried to the ballpark, put on a Terriers uniform, warmed up, and sat on the bench as the afternoon game began.[11] Al Boucher, the Terriers' regular third baseman, was injured early in the game and Cueto replaced him, earning two clean hits and fielding flawlessly.[12]

St. Louis received the two Cubans with a mixture of appreciation and bias. The *St. Louis Star* had greeted Marsans's signing with the question, "Now that we have a Cuban on our team, why not go out and get a Mexican and a Jap, then start a real war on organized baseball?"[13] Cueto's performance, in his debut at third base, elicited the comment that the Terriers should "make a raid on Cuba and steal a dozen more of these dark complicated ball tossers."[14] Another reporter queried, "Now that we have Cueto, why not get Huerta, Villa, Carranza, and Diaz?,"[15] referring to prominent figures in the ongoing Mexican Revolution.

On June 18th, the inevitable happened. A federal marshal approached Marsans in Handlan's Park, asking if he were Armando Marsans. When Marsans responded he was, the marshal handed Marsans a folded piece of paper. Marsans opened the paper. It gave notice that an application for an injunction had been filed to prevent him playing for any team but the Cincinnati Reds and that legal proceedings would follow.[16] Other players had left organized baseball for the new league before Marsans, but Marsans was one of the biggest stars to do so.

Because Marsans was not a U.S. citizen, his trial would be held in a federal court. The ruling in the case would take precedence over all other court decisions in the ongoing struggle in baseball. It would therefore be the biggest battle in the Federal

League–organized baseball war. The rival organizations sent their chief counsels to handle the Marsans case. Arguments for the injunction case were heard at 10 o'clock AM on June 22, in St. Paul, Minnesota, by Judge W.H. Sanborn. Marsans signed an affidavit in St. Louis to be submitted in court in St. Paul so he could continue to play during the court case.[17]

After a brief hearing, Judge Sanborn issued a temporary injunction against Marsans, forcing him to return to the Reds or not play at all:

> We, therefore, in consideration thereof, command you that from and immediately after the receipt and notice of this our writ by you, you shall wholly desist from playing professional baseball during the playing seasons of the years 1914, 1915 and 1916, with any other club or for any person, association, corporation or organization whatsoever.... Hereof fail not.[18]

Sanborn justified his ruling by saying that Marsans's signing with the Reds "made a valid and binding contract, especially after the defendant entered upon the performance of the contract and received the compensation there specified during a part of the term."[19] The Reds were required to post a $13,000 bond to indemnify Marsans for any loss of income if the temporary injunction later was overturned.[20]

This was a serious blow to the Federal League. Though only temporary, the injunction cast doubt on their claim that the ten-day clause lacked mutuality. Still, in the battle for public opinion, the Federal League announced that more than fifty major league players had contacted them since Marsans had signed with the Terriers. Organized baseball, for its part, believed their struggle with the Federal League would soon be over. August Herrmann spoke for the entire organization:

> This decision is the most important of all of our legal victories. Organized baseball has won every case against the Federal League. The independents must now feel convinced that the contracts of organized baseball are above reproach of any kind. I think that this latest decision in the Marsans case will bring players to their senses. The National Commission has decided to bring action against every player who violates his contract obligations. All will be prevented by law from appearing with Federal League clubs.[21]

After the temporary injunction was issued, Marsans was at the center of a flurry of rumors. He denied a report that he had sent a telegram to Cincinnati requesting his remaining possessions be sent to Cuba because he was heading home. On July 2nd, Marsans said, "Although I am not in the game, I am being paid by the St. Louis Federal Club and I expect to stay here."[22]

Prominent baseball writer W.A. Phelon reported that the Reds had all but closed an eight-player deal with the New York Giants that would send Marsans to New York to play for the National League champions. The reporter claimed to have verified the rumors with the Reds' executives. Frank Bancroft, the Reds' business manager, did indeed speak with Marsans on the 6th of July. Marsans told him that he had already accepted advances in the sum of $9,000 from the Terriers and could not return to the Reds even if he wanted to.[23] According to Phelan, Marsans had given his word to Herrmann that if the trade were put through, he would report to New York, return the $9000 to the Terriers,[24] and sign with the Giants for $5,000 per year. The Reds and Giants never consummated the deal.

The date for the hearing to determine if the injunction against Marsans should be made permanent was set for July 8. The court then postponed the hearing; Marsans's case would be heard in September or October, after the court completed the entire criminal docket.[25] With that decision the rest of Armando Marsans's 1914 baseball season disappeared.

Meanwhile, without Marsans, the Reds' promising season was turning into a disaster. *The Sporting News* wrote that their story was "one of long tragedy, brightened only by the fact that the boys fought hard, dying gamely in every lost battle."[26] The Reds would finish last in the National League with a record of sixty and ninety-four, enduring a franchise-record nineteen straight losses at one point. The City of Cincinnati would have to wait five more years for a pennant. Charles Lincoln Herzog would return to John McGraw's Giants in 1916 only to lose another World Series in 1917. Herzog played a total of thirteen seasons in the major leagues compiling an unspectacular .259 lifetime batting average. He died a forgotten man in a hospital in his native Baltimore, having been found in the street, a destitute drunk.

Despite the injunction, the Chicago Cubs were still trying to convince Marsans to join their team. As Clark Griffith had tried to do when he became manager of the Washington Senators, Hank O'Day, former Reds manager, now in charge of the Cubs, wanted

to sign Marsans to his new team. C.H. Thomas, the owner of the
Cubs, was persistent, writing August Herrmann on June 25th,

> I would not care to become involved in a legal tangle, but if
> you can get Marsans to agree to sign with us, and the injunc-
> tion is made permanent, restraining him from playing with the
> Federal League, I will be very glad to consider a trade, which
> will be of benefit to both the Chicago and Cincinnati teams.[27]

The war between the Federal League and organized baseball
was being fought on two fronts: in the court cases and in stadium
attendance. In the former, organized baseball enjoyed the early
triumphs. The Federal League appealed each decision to a higher
court with, for the most part, the same result. The new league,
however, did make inroads with the baseball public and reported
strong attendance for most of its early-season games. Many of the
Federal League franchises built new stadiums to attract fans, the
only remaining example being Chicago's Wrigley Field, originally
known as Weeghman Park. The Chicago Whales (a superlative
example of the Federal League's ridiculous team names) boasted
of triumphs at the turnstiles over their National and American
League rivals in Chicago.

Total attendance was down in the American and National
Leagues, and everywhere teams struggled to make ends meet. The
Federal League produced the most exciting pennant race of the
three leagues, with the Indianapolis Hoosiers winning the pennant by a game and a half. President Gilmore, of the Federal
League, issued a challenge to organized baseball, proposing that
the champions of his league should meet the winner of the
Philadelphia A's–Boston Braves World Series to decide the true
champions of baseball. His challenge went unanswered.

The 1914 season ended among rumors of settlement. Early
November found August "Gerry" Herrmann attempting to build
a consensus among National League owners to accept a peace proposal. The proposal called for one or more of the National League
franchises to be purchased by Federal League owners and the
admittance of other Federal League franchises into the higher
minor leagues. The resolution of the status of players who had
jumped from organized baseball to the Federal League was most
significant to Marsans, and the point proved to be a major road-
block in the negotiations. Several owners favored suspending the
players that, by playing in the Federal League, had violated Rule

20 of the National Agreement. Herrmann, in attempting to convince these men to be more lenient, made an astonishing statement in his communications with National League Executives: "Those who jumped reservations, legally had a right to do so on account of the fact that all the attorneys who have been consulted, were of the unanimous opinion that our old reservation clause was illegal."[28] This admission flatly contradicted organized baseball's adamant defense of the clause in court, a primary reason that Armando Marsans was not allowed to play baseball for most of the 1914 season.

The winter of 1914 and 1915 saw continual reports of the Federal League conflict. With the war metaphor popular due to the bloodshed in Europe, the argot of battle was widely applied to the situation. Headlines referred to the "Belgiumization" of the minor leagues and trench warfare. On January 5, 1915, in an action that brought the baseball war to its "most acute state," the Federal League filed suit against organized baseball under the Sherman Anti-trust Act.

Armando Marsans, circa 1914, probably 26 years old, in a Cincinnati Reds uniform. (Library of Congress)

Judge Kenesaw Mountain Landis presided over the case. Landis, named for the Civil War battle in which his father was injured, was a short energetic man with an unkempt shock of white hair. His reputation as a trustbuster, earned in a 1907 ruling against Standard Oil in which the company was fined $29,240,000 gave the Federal League some hope.[29] What the Federal League may not have known was that Landis was an avid baseball fan. He had grown up in the Midwest, his allegiance torn between the Chicago White Sox and the Chicago Cubs. Many an afternoon found the young Landis sitting in a ballpark, devotedly keeping score.

Among the testimony given by witnesses in the case was Federal Leaguer Mordecai Brown's claim that a manager for the Minneapolis club had once traded a professional ball player for a bulldog. Brown also believed the manager of the St. Louis National League franchise had traded a pitcher for a hunting dog.[30] Both sides rested, awaiting a decision that never came. Landis claimed he was allowing time for the two sides to work out a settlement, which he said would be preferable to him issuing a decision.[31] Some baseball historians speculate that Landis did not rule because the evidence left no option but to find organized baseball in violation of antitrust laws. Such a decision would have rendered all organized baseball contracts, both in the minor leagues and the major leagues, invalid. According to this theory, Landis could not bear to make the decision that guaranteed the destruction of the institution he cherished.

It became clear to the disillusioned public that the most important thing in baseball was the bottom line. The fans felt that they, and the players, were being treated as commodities. One writer, explaining the waning public enthusiasm for the game, wrote: "Professional baseball was in the storm center of a cyclonic disturbance, which transformed the whole thing from a sport to a commercial game. The giant of commercialism dominated the stage and manipulated its puppets until the national game became a business frenzy instead of a popular game."[32]

With the new year came the report that the American League's New York Yankees had been sold for $500,000, then a record for a franchise without a stadium.[33] Despite the Yankees purchase, the financial state of baseball was strained. The national economy was slow. The war in Europe and disenchantment with the game among the public meant that the five top leagues—the Federal League, the American and National leagues, and the two highest minor leagues—

claimed to have lost $1,250,000 dollars in 1914. Only eight clubs in the American and National Leagues were said to be profitable, while five of the eight Federal League teams lost money.[34]

The 1915 season opened with much fanfare. Gilmore announced plans for an expansion of the Federal League to Toronto, Cleveland, Boston, and New York. He reiterated the Federal League's goal: "We do not want to dissolve organized baseball, or the National Commission, and I want to say that we do not seek to join the ranks of organized baseball. We have never asked for it and never will. There is room for three major leagues...."[35] The Indianapolis Hoosiers moved to Newark and became the Peppers in an attempt to tap more of the New York baseball market. Gilmore also moved the Federal League's offices from Chicago to New York to signal the league's new prominence.

Several rules changes were enacted for the 1915 season. Gilmore announced that outfielders who threw their gloves, hats, or any other piece of equipment to stop batted balls would be penalized by granting the batter a home run.[36] Gilmore also banned the "mudball"—a pitch that took dramatic turns because of a piece of dirt, or a clump of sand, stuck to the ball. Pitchers caught throwing a "mudball" would be fined fifty dollars.[37]

In the American League, President Ban Johnson imposed a thirty-day suspension and one hundred dollar fine for the use of "emery balls." An emery ball was a pitch thrown after a pitcher had scuffed the surface of the ball with an emery file so he could get a better grip and cause his pitches to "break" (curve) more.[38] The National League adopted the disabled list, allowing teams to hold players outside of the twenty-one-man roster limit while injured. Presumably, this was done to protect players from being lured to the Federal League.[39]

Rumored settlements between the leagues were frequent throughout the season but peace did not materialize. The *New York Times* reported, "Rumors of peace have been so plentiful that they almost gain credence through repetition, but underneath the surface the baseball war appears to be no nearer settlement than when the outlaw league first established itself."[40]

Baseball Magazine summed up the situation by saying: "Deplore the Federal League if you will, but admit as you must, if you know the facts, that they have fought a game fight, and conducted themselves throughout with all possible respect to the rules of civilized warfare as exemplified in baseball."[41]

8

Resolution

Marsans returned to Cuba for the 1914-1915 winter baseball season, playing for Almendares under an assumed name so as not to jeopardize the status of other Cuban players. According to the rules of the National Agreement, any man who played against a team that fielded a player on organized baseball's ineligible list also became ineligible.

Marsans played an integral role in setting up the St. Louis Terriers' Havana, Cuba, spring training trip for 1915. He corresponded regularly with the St. Louis Terriers management about hotels and training venues. This was the first time that a major league team had chosen Cuba as a spring training location. Marsans greeted Fielder Jones, who had replaced Mordecai Brown as the Terriers manager, at the end of January in Havana, to show him the facilities available to the Terriers. Marsans also helped with the logistics of the training trip, including the scheduling of a series of exhibition games against Cuban baseball teams.[1] "It is the greatest place for the purpose that I have ever laid my eyes on," said Jones. "I don't think there is a better spot in the world to condition a ball club. I have been in a good many places, but Havana has it on all of them."[2]

Rumor in St. Louis had it that the other purpose of Jones's

trip to Havana was to assure that Marsans would stay in the Federal League. Several reports from Cuba claimed that Marsans was weary of his situation and wanted to return to organized baseball. Herrmann received a telegram from James Gaffney of the Boston Nationals saying

> Friend writes me from Cuba/ Marsans is tired of Feds and desires to play with Boston Nationals/ Have I your clubs permission to negotiate with him/ wire me answer to Boston[3]

Another telegram, from the owners of the Yankees, stated:

> Marsans brother has just returned from Havana and states positively that Armando Marsans will remain with Federals unless he can play with Yankees and will play with no other club in organized base ball Is it possible for us to make arrangements with you whereby we can treat him.[4]

And another telegram, from John McGraw of the New York Giants, dated February 23 saying,

> ...Saw Marsans Friday in Havana he said he would not play for the St. Louis Nationals because of Federal League contract/ New York club would like to have him/ what is your best proposition should we come to an agreement/ would want Marsans to go back to Cincinnati and then be transferred to us to avoid legal complications/ am going south/ rush answer[5]

Fielder Jones reported that Miller Huggins, manager of the Cardinals, had been to see Marsans three times offering him everything to come back to organized baseball. Marsans's answer was always the same: He would not leave the St. Louis Terriers.

After Huggins's advances had been rebuffed, the Boston Braves tried to acquire Marsans. They offered him the same salary he was making with the Terriers, a $2000 signing bonus, and the promise to repay the Terriers what they had paid Marsans. Marsans's responded at length, and his reply makes clear what none of the businessmen in organized baseball had been able to understand- that the issue of honor was paramount to Marsans:

> I am bound to the St. Louis Federals by my honor, and it would take much more than the National League could offer to get

me to turn traitor to men who have treated me grandly, as have Mr. Ball and Mr. Stifel....

I told the gentleman from Boston that it was an impossibility for me to have any dealings whatever with him. I explained to him that the matter was purely one of honor—not of money.

I have never regretted my action in turning down the offer at any time and I probably never will. I never had known what it was like to receive good, fair, clean treatment from a club owner or manager until I reached St. Louis, and I am eager to show my appreciation of the royal consideration I have been shown there....

The only thing that worries me now is whether or not I will be able to play center field for Jones this year. I know that the St. Louis club owners did not get the worth of their money out of me last year and I am anxious to make good their loss, if such is possible.

I want the St. Louis fans, as well as the club owners, to know that I am loyal to my friends. I have no ambition to be taken back into the folds of the National League, my ambition is to win the pennant for Ball and Stifel. They have treated me as I was never treated before and I intend to give them every ounce of baseball there is in me in return.[6]

On the afternoon of March 2nd, the eighteen players on the Terriers team, their manager, and several reporters from St. Louis settled into the Hotel Gran America in Havana. The players' days began at 7:30 A.M. as ordered by Fielder Jones with the tinkle of the small bell in each room, manually rung from the front desk. The team came downstairs in ones and twos and ate a large breakfast at the training table.

Cuban Customs refused, without explanation, to clear the trunk containing the Terriers's uniforms and equipment until midday on the 3rd, forcing the Terriers to cancel their first morning practice. This was Jones's first spring training with the Terriers, and he was determined to establish a pattern of hard work. For two and a half hours that afternoon, the Terriers took batting practice, fielded balls, practiced throwing and ran sprints. The field was to everyone's liking and it was generally held by the players to be the equal of any in the United States.[7] At the end of practice Jones told his men to run the mile and a half back to the hotel.[8]

Jones was a man of discipline, pushing his men to perfect the skills and master the small details of the game. Be it bunting, fielding, or relaying the ball from the outfield, Jones demanded his players understand the game's subtleties.

Jones favored the "hook" slide. Instead of sliding directly at the base as is common today, in a "hook slide" the runner tries to keep as much of his body away from the base and the defensive player as possible. He slides on one hip, hooking the opposite leg away from him, touching the base with only the foot of his hooked leg. He ordered his players to spend much of their practice time in the sliding pits perfecting their technique.

The extent of Marsans's fame in Cuba surprised the Terriers players. Walking in the street or seated in a restaurant, the people of Havana often waved or said hello to him and it seemed he was "a much greater favorite than the President of the island."[9] The cigar-smoking members of the team purchased many Fabrica Tobacos de A. Marsans y Ca. cigars and took pleasure in smoking them.

Though Cuba was a popular vacation destination for Americans, the Terriers spring training brought many of the players to the island for the first time. Accounts of their experiences written by the St. Louis reporters reveal the ignorance and misconceptions held by average Americans regarding Cuban culture:

> Everybody down here speaks Spanish. Now and then one will find a native who speaks English. To date this has proven to be one of the most difficult problems [of] the ballplayers of the St. Louis Federal League squad.[10]

Of course everyone in Cuba spoke Spanish. The fact that this seemed worthy of comment to one reporter implies a lack of awareness at best, and an indelible ethnocentric view of the world at worst. Frequently the tone of the articles intimated that the facts about Cuban culture were different from the prevailing ideas that Americans held:

> St. Louisans, or, for that matter, citizens of any other big city in the States, would surely be surprised if told that Havana is as up to date and hustling in its methods as any place in the universe.[11]

The misconception that Havana was not a modern city may have been the product of the renewed focus on the debate of race relations in the United States. While the questions and tensions surrounding the assimilation of the African-American community continued to haunt the United States, immigration proved to be a new catalyst for race thinking. In 1907, John R. Commons published his book *Races and Immigrants in America*. Commons stated, "Race differences are established in the very blood and physical constitution. They are difficult to eradicate, and they yield only to the slow processes of the centuries. Races may change their religions, their forms of government, their modes of industry, and their languages, but underneath all these changes there may continue physical, mental, and moral incapacities which determine the real character of their religion, government, industry, and literature."[12]

Commons thought the true foundations of democracy were in the individuals that constituted a nation. These people must have intelligence, self-respect, self-control, and an ability to maintain their rights. Many of the newly arrived peasants from Europe, especially Southern and Eastern Europe, were, in Commons's view, lacking in the qualities which were necessary for democracy, for they "had been reduced to the qualities similar to those of an inferior race that favors despotism and oligarchy rather than democracy. The Spaniards and the French were accustomed to paternal governments and therefore as a people did not have the self-reliance and capacity for sustained exertion."[13]

In the hierarchy of races, the ability to self-govern was developing into the standard by which peoples were admitted into the society of "civilized" nations. The Mexican Revolution and the unrest in Cuba and other parts of Latin America proved that Latinos did not meet this standard. "No longer were Americans in general being characterized primarily by their adherence to a set of political and social ideals allegedly representing the universal aspirations of all humanity, but democracy itself was beginning to be defined as racial in origin and thus realizable perhaps only by people with certain hereditary traits."[14]

After a week of practicing twice a day in the warm Cuban sunshine, the Terriers began a series of games with Marsans's Almendares team and its rivals, Habana. The Cubans were in top form, having played together for the entire winter season. The Terriers, under Jones, won their first game and then the second in eleven innings against Almendares, with Marsans playing centerfield for his Federal League team.

Though the Terriers would win nine of the eleven contests they played against local teams, all the games were closely contested and many were decided by one run. The Cubans' high standard of play garnered much praise from the Americans:

> Victory over the Cubans at this early stage in the training is not anything of which to make light. Every Cuban fielder is equipped with an arm of steel, it is virtually impossible to take an extra base on them when on an ordinary team it would be easy. The Cubans seem to know instinctively where to throw the ball: in short, they seldom if ever have been known to make a "bone" play. The right thing at the right time seems second nature with them.[15]

In particular, the Terriers had enormous respect for Almendares star pitcher José Méndez, "who would have been in the big leagues long since had it not been for his color."[16] In an article in a St. Louis paper subtitled "Cuban Is Blacker Than the Ace of Spades, but He Surely Can Pitch" the writer expressed his awe at Méndez's ability to pick runners off first base. No one questioned if the motion were permissible, but everyone was impressed by its swiftness. Jones was so impressed that he urged his pitchers to try to adapt Méndez's motion to their pick-off moves.[17]

The praise was not limited to Méndez. In an article titled "Throwing Arms of Cuban Stars Are Best in the Game," one St. Louis reporter wrote, "There is no club in the major leagues today which can produce a trio of outfielders with as powerful and accurate a set of arms as these natives possess.... For throwing, at least, these dusky ball tossers will outstrip any other club in the world."[18]

Praise for the Cubans' on-field abilities was tempered by subtle manifestations of the belief in Americans' intellectual superiority. "The people of Havana are not dull by any means. They are picking up much American slang and are witty when they learn a little English."[19] Though the second sentence is complementary, the observation taken as a whole reveals a perception, presumed to be shared by the reporter's readers, that Cubans were "dull."

The same preconception of inferior mental capacity is evident in the following review of the Cuban players, which acknowledges their physical ability, but suggests that they were incapable of thinking on their own:

> The Cubans play a very clever game, and, no doubt, if they were led by an able manager, would prove the equal of any club in the United States. Each man is a natural-born player, and it is only the lack of systematized attack which loses games for them. The material is there, and, if they had the teacher, they would form a wonderful club. There are three Negroes on the club and the remaining men are Cubans.[20]

In the final sentence, the writer reveals, again, the prevalence of the view that only the players of purely European descent qualified as citizens.

The Terriers closed camp with a 4–3 victory over Almendares and left for St. Louis via Key West and Jacksonville on the 5th of April. Cuba was declared an exceptional site for spring training. The weather had been nearly perfect, with the Terriers losing only a handful of practice sessions to rain. Though occasionally too hot, the warm weather was pointed to as one of the major reasons the team had not suffered any injuries.

The Terriers' stay in Havana opened the eyes of more people to the potential of Cubans as professional baseball players. One reporter said farewell to Cuba by writing:

> Sporting men in Havana are of the opinion Cuba will send more men to the big leagues and produce more championship athletes in proportion to its population than any other state or country in the world, as soon as athletics advance a bit more. Already baseball has reached a stage where it is played more universally than in the States. On every lot—and there are a few of them—are groups of coming greats who throw, catch, bat and talk baseball with all the graceful motions and more nonchalance and insouciance than the American boy.[21]

Despite their productive spring training in Havana, the Terriers began the 1915 regular season poorly. The Federal League realized Jones's squad was losing too consistently to win favor with St. Louis fans, and that something had to be done to assure the franchise would draw fans.[22] The situation became so serious that the president of the Federal League came to St. Louis to confer with the owners.

Manager Jones knew one answer to the dilemma. He pleaded with Terriers' owner Philip Ball to find a way to get Marsans into the game. Ball, taking his manager's request to heart, met with an attorney from organized baseball. The injunction against Marsans playing for anyone but the Reds still stood at the beginning of the 1915 season. Ball proposed that if organized baseball would agree to waive the injunction against Marsans, the Federal League would permit organized baseball to withdraw the $13,000 bond held to compensate the Terriers if the temporary injunction against Marsans were overruled. Marsans would be free to play with the Terriers until the court decided his permanent fate. The talks widened to include the fates of other players who had left organized baseball for the Federal League but the negotiations collapsed because organized baseball refused to compromise on the specific issue of Marsans. Their obstinance was probably due to the opinions of several of the hardline owners in organized baseball who felt that those players who had joined the Federal League should never be pardoned.

Concurrent with Ball's attempts to get Marsans back on the field, the St. Louis Cardinals announced they had acquired the rights to Marsans; If the courts ordered Marsans to return to organized baseball, he would play for the Cardinals, not the Cincinnati Reds.

After the negotiations with organized baseball failed, the Terriers persisted in trying to find a way for Marsans to return to the field. Federal League lawyers again attempted to have Marsans's case decided in the St. Louis Federal Court. Before the St. Louis Federal Court even had fixed a date, many of the figures in the Marsans case received subpoenas. At the beginning of May, Dwight Currie, Marsans's lawyer, deposed a number of key figures: first Marsans, then St. Louis Terriers officials, and then Frank Bancroft, the Cincinnati Reds business manager. The secretary of the St. Louis Cardinals confirmed that his team had secured the rights to Marsans in a trade with the Reds. The Cardinals' president corroborated the information.

Charles Herzog, still manager of the Reds, despite their disastrous 1914 season, was the last to be deposed. In what must have been a tense room, Marsans and others listened as Herzog responded to Currie's questions. Herzog proved to be the most difficult deponent. He stated he was unsure about the trade with the Cardinals, or any decisions regarding what would happen to Marsans if he were to return to the Reds. After his deposition, Herzog rose, walked over to Marsans, and extended his hand. The two former teammates shook hands and Herzog urged Marsans to forget their past differences.[23]

It would have been hard for Marsans to forget what sort of man Herzog was. In the prior day's game between the Reds and the Cardinals in St. Louis, Herzog had exploded at the umpire over a controversial call and the umpire ejected him. The manager returned to the Reds bench but reemerged to continue arguing with the umpire. It is not clear what followed, but manager Herzog and home plate umpire Cy Rigler ended up in a fistfight at home plate.

Both men were arrested after the game and appeared in court on peace disturbance charges.[24] It is the manager's responsibility to challenge umpires and even to get ejected from a game on occasion to motivate his team, but in this case Herzog crossed the line. He had placed himself before the team, the very same crime of which he had accused Marsans.

With Marsans still unable to take the field, the Terriers could not afford to bring him on their road trips. When they were traveling, Marsans practiced each day at Handlan's Park from 10 to 11 A.M. Sometimes he worked out with other players, but most days found Marsans running sprints or practicing his throwing alone in the deserted stadium. "Marsans will probably deteriorate more rapidly from want of competitive play than he would from age. If he has another season of bench-warming to go through without work he will be completely forgotten."[25]

Marsans spoke about his plight:

> The other day I go to [Philip] Ball and say, "I'm tired of taking your money. Let me join the Cardinals and I come back if Judge says so. I want to play ball." But Ball he say, "I'm no kicking about your money am I?" so what am I gonna do? Jess stay here and do nothing, I guess, because I can't leave square fellows like these. I like to go back now to the Reds and play ball, even after what Herzog said, because I like baseball first, but never will I quit these people. They're too square. I no sleep at night. Just think and think. I say to myself, what if the Feds lose and nobody wants me? It worries me when I think I might not play ball never again. Sometimes I get seck.[26]

Having failed in their attempt to have the case transferred to the St. Louis Federal Court, Federal League attorneys appeared before Judge Landis in Chicago on June 28th, asking him to dissolve the temporary injunction prohibiting Marsans from playing. The lawyers pointed out that when Marsans jumped to the Federal League and was enjoined, sixteen other players had also been temporarily enjoined from playing for making similar moves. In June 1915, more than a year later, Marsans was the only one of the seventeen players who was still prohibited from playing. Landis declined to dissolve the injunction issued by Judge Sanborn, but he did allow the Federal League to file an intervening petition by which the Marsans case would be decided with the other cases. Landis promised an early decision in the matter.[27]

But Landis continued to stall. July became August and he did not rule. The Federal League realized Landis was going to take as long as possible and, frustrated, threatened to start raiding the rosters of organized baseball if Landis did not decide the case. On August 10, Marsans, through his attorney, petitioned the Federal District Court in St. Louis to modify or dissolve the injunction.[28] Representing Marsans was C.C. Madison, the same man who, more than a year ago, had twice attempted to entice the Cuban to leave the Reds for the Federal League.

Madison chose a three-pronged legal strategy to prove Marsans's injunction was no longer valid. First, he contended that the Cincinnati Exhibition Company had failed to fulfill its part of the contract as required by the preliminary injunction, in that after Marsans had jumped to the Federal League the Reds no longer had any intention of allowing Marsans to play for them. The Reds countered by entering as evidence a letter from Herrmann to Marsans written on June 27, 1914, which concluded:

> The above facts are recited and this letter is written for the purpose of again advising you that The Cincinnati Exhibition Company is ready and willing at all times to observe and carry out in good faith all the terms and conditions of its contract with you, and on behalf of The Cincinnati Exhibition Company I urge you to return to The Cincinnati Base Ball Club and resume your place on the team. We have no player to fill your position and there is no opportunity for us to find a man of your extraordinary ability to fill the place made vacant by your absence.[29]

Marsans denied having received the letter, but the Reds produced a receipt for the letter bearing Marsans's signature. Madison attempted to minimize the damage to Marsans's credibility by arguing that the Cuban was ineligible to play for the Reds, or any other team in organized baseball, because he had taken the field for the Terriers. Rule 20 of the National Agreement states that a player who plays for an "outlaw" team is ineligible for three years unless he petitions the National Commission.[30] Madison therefore dismissed Herrmann's letter as "merely a self-serving piece of evidence concocted for the sole purpose of pretense. Good faith is not represented in a single syllable of it."[31]

Madison's second point was that the contract Marsans had signed with Cincinnati only bound him for the 1914 season. The standard organized baseball contract contained several blank spaces in which were typed the agreed duration of the contract. In article eight of Marsans's contract with the Reds, the blank space, inexplicably, contained only "1914" instead of "1914–1916," as had been entered in the other spaces in the contract. Madison seized upon this secretarial error as evidence that Marsans should now be free to play for whatever team he chose.

Madison's third point was one of the primary arguments in all Federal League cases. He contended that organized baseball's contracts were illegal, and therefore non-binding, due to the lack of mutuality in the ten-day clause.

On August 19th, Judge David Dyer ruled that the injunction was no longer in effect and Marsans was free to play.[32] He based his decision on Madison's second point, the failure to include the years 1915 and 1916 in one space in Marsans's contract. The court ordered that Marsans was free play for Cincinnati or any other team during the remainder of the year 1915 and 1916. The ruling was technically a modification, not a dissolution, of the injunction, nullifying the part of the original ruling that prohibited Marsans from playing in 1915 and 1916.[33]

Philip Ball, who was in court when Dyer announced his decision, described Marsans's reaction: "Judge Dyer's decision hit him like a pardon would a life-termer. I never saw anybody quite so happy as Marsans after hearing the decision."[34]

On the 19th of August, Marsans left St. Louis on the noon train to join the Terriers in Brooklyn.[35] The Terriers' poor performance had begun to improve by early June. Their pitching staff drew rave reviews and the defense, especially the infield, was as good as any team's. The Terriers were playing Jones's brand of baseball, and it was working. "The teamwork of Jones's club excels by far that of any championship aggregation baseball has known in recent years."[36] They were in the thick of the Federal League pennant race, only 2½ games behind leaders Newark and Chicago.

Marsans returned to the lineup on August 21st. Unfortunately, in his fourth game back he was badly spiked in the leg and had to have the wound stitched. The injury forced Marsans to miss several games. When he returned to the field, the Terriers put together a stretch run for the pennant, but Marsans was unable

to contribute. In 36 games, the Cuban batted .177—22 hits in 124
at bats. with only five stolen bases.

The St. Louis Terriers, with a record of 87–67, tied the
Chicago Whales, who won 86 games and lost 66, but the Whales
were awarded the pennant for their slightly better winning percentage. How many times must Marsans have asked himself what
would have happened had he been able to perform at his pre-
courtcase level?

9

In the American League

By the end of 1915, the Federal League had run its course. Though some owners were willing to continue the fight, most had grown weary, losing considerable sums of money. Gilmore went to the National League leadership hoping for a settlement. All involved knew the outlaw league was surrendering, and the move was a relief to many in the organized baseball.

The settlement, reached in the last days of 1915, permitted Federal League owners to sell players back to organized baseball. The accord repaid some of the Federal League losses by buying the Brooklyn Federal League Park. It also allowed Charles Weeghman, owner of the Chicago Whales, to purchase the Chicago Cubs. The Pittsburgh franchise was purchased for $50,000. The Kansas City and Buffalo franchises were insolvent and had been supported financially in secret by the other owners in the Federal League for much of the 1915.[1]

The Federal League agreed to withdraw the anti-trust suit it had brought against organized baseball, which still remained undecided in Judge Landis' hands. Landis closed the legal proceedings by stating: "The Court's expert knowledge of baseball, obtained by more than thirty years of observation of the game as a spectator, convinced me that if an order had been entered it would have been, if not destructive, at least vitally injurious to the game of baseball."[2] The accord was signed with the agreement that the financial settlement of the Federal League's Baltimore franchise situation would be determined afterwards to everyone's satisfaction. The Baltimore franchise owners were never satisfied. They brought their own legal action against organized baseball. Ironically, it was this case, an extension of the Federal League, which galvanized organized baseball's monopoly; in 1922, when the Supreme Court heard the case, the court ruled baseball was a unique institution, and was therefore exempt from the anti-trust legislation.

Because Marsans's permission to play had been only a modification of the injunction, representatives of the former Federal League and organized baseball asked for, and received, a dismissal of the Cincinnati Exhibition Company versus Armando Marsans case.[3] Marsans's case and status were finally settled after nineteen months. Philip Ball, owner of the former Terriers team, purchased the St. Louis Browns and brought his best players, including Armando Marsans, and Manager Fielder Jones with him to the Browns.

A combination of the strong Terriers team, which nearly won the 1915 Federal League pennant, and the old St. Louis Browns team proved too much of a temptation for those inclined to pick pennant winners before a season starts. Fielder Jones said, "I'm going south with the best club it ever has been my privilege to manage. I have a team that is as good as any in the American League, and the American League has a higher standard this year than ever before in its history ... the material is here and it's up to me."[4]

The Browns chose Palestine, Texas, as their base for spring training. The team arrived in Palestine on the last day of February, having left St. Louis in a snowstorm. Marsans received permission from Fielder Jones to report to training camp two weeks late, because the Cuban season did not finish until after the opening of the Browns' camp. He would join the Browns in Houston on March 11th as they made their way back to St. Louis.

Yet again, Marsans failed to join his team as agreed, and as before, he sent no communication to explain his absence. Marsans had impressed Jones with his determination and smart baseball in his short and unsuccessful return to the Terriers at the end of the 1915 season, but the memory did not save Marsans in his delinquency. Jones, with a full, healthy lineup, saw no need to hold a position for Marsans in the outfield.

When a reporter remarked what a great player Marsans was, Jones responded, "What good is a good player who does not show up?"[5]

On their last night in Palestine, the Browns attended a farewell dance. When their curfew of 11 o'clock drew near, the women at the dance convinced the players to ask Jones if they could stay out until midnight. The players sent an envoy to their manager, who replied, "We came down here to play ball, not to dance." The players were all in their rooms by 11 o'clock.[6]

On March 8th, 1916, only a few hundred miles to the west of the Browns' training camp, Pancho Villa and a band of Mexicans crossed the U.S.-Mexican border and attacked the town of Columbus, New Mexico, 65 miles west of El Paso. The raid made headlines around the country. Columbus was a town of six hundred people enjoying a minor boom as the result of nearby oil discoveries. The Thirteenth United States Cavalry was encamped at Columbus and quickly responded to Villa's raid. The engagement was fought among burning buildings, set afire by Villa's men, and lasted almost two hours.

For much of Marsans's time in the United States, Mexico was devouring itself in the Mexican Revolution. The conflict provided a steady flow of stories and images in U.S. newspapers over nearly ten years of violent unrest and struggle in Mexico. It is difficult to quantify the effect the Revolution and reporting of the event had on the image that Americans held of Latinos.

Villa's raid was one more event in a seemingly endless continuum of violence, made more impressive by the boldness of the plan to extend the conflict onto American soil. Many interpreted Villa's act as the antithesis of civilized behavior and a manifestation of the inferior characteristics of the Latino temperament. It was proof that Mexicans—and by extension all Latin Americans—were incapable of lawful self-rule.

Soon after the raid, a member of the Thirteenth Cavalry came to visit the Browns, hoping to recruit several ballplayers into the army for what he believed was imminent war with Mexico. He believed baseball players were perfectly suited as "bomb throwers."

When asked what the army salary was, the officer replied $13.65 per month. One of the Browns said he turned down an offer from the Federal League in 1915 for $1000 dollars per month. The Army did not recruit any men from the Browns.[7]

Marsans was still missing on the 16th of March, when Jones finally received a letter, saying his tardiness was due to the fact his father was ill. This did not sit well with Jones. Jones issued an ultimatum from Memphis, Tennessee, where the Browns had stopped, that Marsans was to report to St. Louis on the 24th of March or face the consequences. But Marsans's last game was played on the 23rd, making it impossible to arrive on time.

Marsans arrived in St. Louis on March 28th. He went to Sportsman's Park, deposited his equipment, greeted other players at the park, and sat down to a ten-cent poker game in the clubhouse. "I have been playing ball for the past two months and I'm in shape to jump right in, if Fielder wants me. Because of sickness at home, I was unable to join the club in Texas. However, my lack of practice in Texas will not be a handicap to me here, because I have kept in shape throughout the winter."[8]

The Browns team was among the fastest in the American League. Some of the players, however, lacked experience and knowledge or were not familiar with the finer points of the game as Jones wanted them played. One of these subtleties pertained to the outfielders, and Marsans in particular. During a practice session in early April, Marsans was stationed in center field. The batter hit a "Texas leaguer," or a softly hit ball that goes just over the infielders' reach and into the outfield. Lavan, the shortstop, turned his back to the plate and ran into the outfield to try to catch the ball. Marsans sprinted in but slowed down because he saw the infielder running out to catch the ball. The ball fell in for a hit. When the side was retired, Marsans ran back into the bench, Jones asked him about the play and the Cuban explained he thought Lavan would make the play.

"You outfielders will have to take more chances on short flies than you do," replied Jones. "You would have made an easy catch of that ball if you continued to come in. Less Texas leaguers will drop behind the infield if you fellows take more chances and attempt to make a catch."

"Well, if I continued running," said the Cuban, "I might have collided with Lavan and either or both of us might have been injured."

"Nothing of the sort," Jones said in response, and he explained to Marsans that the field captain was responsible for calling the play and that it was much easier for the outfielder, coming in toward the ball, to make the play than for the infielder to try to catch the ball over his shoulder running away from home plate.

Marsans conceded he had been wrong. In a subsequent inning, the batter hit a similar "Texas leaguer." Lavan turned and dashed toward the outfield to make the catch. Marsans charged hard from center field. The field captain called for Marsans to make the play. Lavan stopped, while Marsans continued running and made the catch.[9]

The Browns' pre-season culminated in a spring series with the St. Louis Cardinals. The four-game series divided not only the city of St. Louis but also Cuba. Miguel González, the Cuban catcher who had played with Marsans for the Cincinnati Reds in 1914, was now a Cardinal. In the second game of the intra-city battle, Marsans's two hits, half of his team's total, were a clean single and an infield hit, which he beat out with his still exceptional speed. The game was scoreless through eight innings. In the ninth, the Cardinals brought in four runs, two of them scoring when Marsans misjudged a short hit from his position in center field.

Marsans's misplay and the difficult end to his 1915 season did not deter a former Browns scout from effusive praise of Marsans. After watching him perform for the first time in the Browns-Cardinals series, the former scout said:

> Marsans is my idea of a great ballplayer. I like the way he steps into the ball and I like the way he runs the bags. He is one of the fastest runners I have ever seen on the ball field, and he seems to possess all the natural qualities that a great ballplayer should have.

The scout was especially impressed with how quickly Marsans got out of the batter's box when he hit the ball.[10] In close plays at first base, the fraction of a second lost in a slow start from the batter's box is often the difference between a hit and an out.

In the third game of the series with the Cardinals, Jones's nine trailed the Cardinals 2–0 at the end of eight innings. The Cardinals' pitcher had allowed only two hits. Marsans came to the plate in the top of the ninth. He scraped around in the dirt in the batter's box, then settled in, shifting back and forth as he waited for the pitch. Marsans drove the ball down the right field line into the corner. He was out of the box at the crack of the bat, running at top speed within a few strides. Three bases were his for the taking. He sped around first and then second, arriving at third, easily safe. The hit sparked a rally that scored Marsans and three other Browns in a victorious ninth inning. Marsans hit .308 in the series against the Cardinals and earned himself a place in the starting lineup. Jones had been angry with Marsans for reporting late but he was so fond of Marsans's knowledge of the game and determination that he chose to start the Cuban for the beginning of the regular season.

On April 12th, opening day of the 1916 season, the Browns beat the Indians in Cleveland in front of a capacity crowd. Young George Sisler had found a home at first base, Del Pratt was at second and Charlie Deal at third. The light-hitting "Doc" Lavan played shortstop and Grover Hartley was catching. In the outfield Burt Shotton, in left, and Jack Tobin, in right, flanked Marsans.

Despite their opening-day win, the beginning of the Browns's 1916 season was not good. Jones made changes including dropping Marsans, who was batting just .216 at the end of April,[11] from fourth to sixth in the batting order. There seemed to be rising sentiment against Marsans in St. Louis. "Who is the gentleman who started this story that Marsans is a great ball player? Somebody has a whole lot of blame to shoulder. Marsans didn't show a thing last year when he broke into the lineup for the Federals. His hitting was pitiful. They told us that his batting eye had been dimmed by his long stay on the bench.... Isn't it about time the Cuban showed something or is it possible that he has no goods to display?"[12] But Marsans began to turn his season around. In one game against the Yankees on May 22, Marsans got three hits in four plate appearances, including an inside-the-park home run. He drove in three runs, scored twice, and stole a base in the Browns' 9–5 victory. He also made "the prettiest play seen in New York thus far this season when he plucked Pipp's liner off his shoe tops and did a graceful somersault in the seventh."[13] By June 9th, Marsans had raised his average to .255, 39th in the American League. Only nine players were batting above .300 at that time.[14]

In one of these games, a Browns runner was heading toward third base looking to score on his teammate's hit, but Jones stopped the man at third. Sitting on the bench Marsans said, "Rotten work, Jones."

That night in the hotel Jones was walking down the hallway and, seeing Marsans, stopped him.

"Marsans," Jones began, "did I hear you shout 'rotten' when I stopped that man at third today?"

"Sure—it was rotten," responded Marsans.

"Well, perhaps you were right. But I want to show you why I think you were wrong." Jones then explained to Marsans why he had made the decision. After the explanation he asked Marsans: "Now you agree with me don't you?"

"It was rotten, that's all," said the Cuban.[15]

Marsans was willing to listen to Jones, and in the case of charging in to catch "Texas leaguers," was willing to admit he had been wrong, but in other cases, Marsans exceptional understanding of the game gave him the confidence to stick by his judgment of a play.

Jones was demanding, but he also nurtured players to get the best out of them, as seen in both cases with Marsans. "Pictured as a relentless driver and martinet. Jones is neither. He lectures his men to tears at times in the clubhouse; he 'calls' them on the bench or coaching line; he keeps watch on them like a human time-clock, to see that they keep their hours; and he can sting with sarcasm.... But he also knows how to pat his men on the back, give credit for deserving plays, listen to reasonable arguments and defend his men against critics like a world's championship alibi merchant."[16]

Despite Jones's leadership, the talented Browns slipped into last place by late May due to a lack of cohesion on the field. Their bad record was not bringing people to the stadiums, home or away. Owner Phil Ball was undeterred. He was willing to spend more money to get still more talent to turn his ball club around. Ball wired Fielder Jones in Philadelphia that he had $50,000 in the bank at Jones's disposal if he wanted to buy new players.[17] As in any team sport, individual stars in baseball seldom lead a franchise to success. It is, instead, the team that forms a unit, encompassing all of its players, that becomes stronger than the sum of its parts and is most likely to achieve greatness. Jones understood this and declined Ball's offer, believing he could make his team into a successful entity without additional talent.

The same optimism was expressed about Marsans: "Marsans always looks good, but he simply can't get going at the bat. The Cuban has the spunk, the pluck, the gimp and can't be kept from scoring runs. He looks like a great ballplayer, even if he is hitting 80 points below his true form. He surely is a comfort on fly balls, and on the bases, while even when he is not hitting he always looks as if he is going to knock down the fence. He will pretty soon."[18]

On June 5th, after four wins in a row, it seemed as though the Browns were finally coalescing. It was Marsans who had the game-winning hit and the *St. Louis Globe-Democrat* said, "The Cuban is a good ballplayer and it is against all baseball precedent that he should slump to playing the ball he did last fall and this spring. Marsans is still well below the age limit at which players go back and he appears just as good an athlete now as when he ranked with the great outfielders while playing at Cincinnati. Yesterday's hit may or may not be the start of his return to form, but this is almost certain to come sooner or later."[19]

In the heat of an extra-inning battle against the Yankees, Marsans made an excellent catch of a deep fly to left-centerfield in the twelfth. In the bottom of the inning, he seemingly beat out an infield hit sliding into first base, but was called out. Marsans argued his case and the umpire ejected him. Bill Evans, the umpire, wired a report of the incident to the president of the American League, Ban Johnson, who immediately declared Marsans suspended for three games. Marsans reported that he said nothing to the umpire. "He so surprise me that I jump up and down. I no control myself. I'm safe, he say out. What would you do?" said Marsans.

"Marsans said nothing offensive to me," said Evans. "At least if he did I didn't hear him. However, actions speak louder than words. He tried to show me up by falling into a feigned faint. I won't stand for that. Had he told me, so that only myself and those in the immediate vicinity could hear, that my decision was damned rotten, I would have argued the point with him. But he didn't do that. He did something the fans could readily interpret."

The unwritten rules that govern interactions between players and umpires deem the action of showing-up an umpire as punishable by ejection. A three-game suspension seems extreme for Marsans's action but Marsans bears some blame for the incident. His feigned feint at the absurdity of Evans's call was an action that probably would have been permitted on a Cuban diamond, but Marsans lost sight of his surroundings, and acted in a manner offensive to the American umpire.

The timing was unfortunate for Marsans, for he had been hitting well prior to the incident. Several times in the season Marsans seemed on the edge of regaining his batting ability. He hit well for three or four consecutive games and then fell flat. On the 15th of June, Marsans showed his ability. He had three timely hits in four plate appearances and scored two runs. Marsans also made an outstanding catch in the outfield eliciting the comment that "Hall of fame outfielder Speaker, or no other man, has played a better field than Marsans has played this season."[20]

Marsans was a student of the game, constantly observing the players and the plays. He was not afraid to voice his opinion about strategy. During one game Marsans recommended that Jones let the speedier Tobin run for Severeid after Severeid got to first base in a close game. Jones shook his head and Marsans sat down. After the next batter got a hit, moving Severid to second, Jones reconsidered and made the substitution Marsans had suggested, substantially increasing the Browns's chance to score.[21]

Meanwhile, in a game on July 17th against the New York Giants, Marsans's fellow Cuban, Miguel González, was part of an incident that demonstrated perceptions of Latinos. González doubled in the eighth inning with two out. The next Cardinal batter singled to left. González rounded third and headed home. The throw from the left fielder arrived well before González. The Giants' catcher waited for the Cuban at the plate. González tried to free the ball from the catcher's hand by hitting it with his knee. Brad Kocher, the Giants' catcher, responded after the play by calling González a "nigger." González responded with Spanish expletives and two other players had to prevent González and Kocher from fighting at home plate.

Accounts vary about what happened after the game but the two players ended up fighting. One paper said González easily won the fight while another may have invented an account in which a vanquished González went to the dressing room and returned, with a weapon. "Testimony of eye-witnesses differ as to the nature of Miguel's equipment but whatever it was, it flashed in the evening sun."[22] All accounts agree the fight was broken up. Kocher charged González with assault. González quickly countered by charging Kocher with the same.

Police arrived at some point in the altercation and the two players were put in the back seat of the Cardinals' owner's car. Manager Huggins sat between González and Kocher on the car ride to the police station, and policeman rode in front seat, next to the chauffeur. Charges were entered but tempers had subsided during the car ride and the charges were immediately and mutually withdrawn.[23]

There is no evidence that González brandished a knife or any other type of weapon in the fight but the reporting revealed an exaggeration in line with views of Latinos as quick tempered, and likely to react in an overly violent manner. What is most interesting about the González incident is that it reveals the incapacity of the majority of Americans, at least as represented by the press, to comprehend the actions of foreigners. In their confusion, they revert to habituated conceptions of those they do not understand and in so doing they reinforce the stereotypes with what they perceive, and remember to be, factual evidence.

Soon after the incident the *St. Louis Post-Dispatch* writers broached the issue of race, temperament, and sport:

> Many are the discussions that have arisen over questions of physical superiority of this or that race over another, or over the rest of the world. Discussions of the sort are futile because the respective races have neither the same opportunities for development nor an equal number of men to pick from.
> Among many the delusion exists that temperamental differences of race make for efficiency. Members of the white race are especially guilty of this sophistry. They pat themselves on the back and think themselves the chosen people, physically and mentally.
> As a matter of fact the white race includes about every variety of temperament known.[24]

The article clearly outlines the prevailing views of the issues and also shows that the populace of the United States was not of one opinion about the issue of ethnicity and inherent ability. These contrary opinions did not frequently appear in the mainstream press in Marsans's era, and if writings in newspapers reflect the opinions of the people, it may be concluded that only a small minority of people held these points of view.

A heat wave descended upon St. Louis in mid-summer and aggravated the frustrations of the Browns. To battle the heat Marsans and pitcher Eddie Plank bought army cots and set them up on the top deck of the grandstand, where the open air and breezes provided comfort during the hot nights. Soon a small colony of Browns had established itself at the ballpark. "The only danger attached to this," said Plank, "is the possibility of being blown away." The arrangement must have made it difficult for

Marsans to keep up his appearance, but he seems to have succeeded. "Marsans is by all odds the neatest dresser among the Brown players. The Cuban is always immaculately groomed, affects grays, always has his linen perfectly laundered, wears a beautiful set of old-fashioned shirt buttons; in a word, follows the advice of Polonius, and maintains an attire 'neat, but not gaudy.'"[25]

Marsans had upped his batting average to .252 by June 11th. It went as high as .272 on June 25th, placing him 24th in the American League, but there it reached a plateau, well below what he had accomplished in Cincinnati. At the end of June, he was batting .256.

"I never saw such a season for slumps," said Marsans. "Just as soon as I get out of one batting slump I get into another. It makes me sick."[26] Marsans claimed he did not notice any difference in the pitching quality between the American and National leagues. "Because I have not hit as heavily in the American as I hit in the National I have been told that the former is the fast league. I hit less in the Federal League than I am hitting in the American League. On that basis the Federal would have been faster than the American.

"Hitting," Marsans continued, "is largely a matter of luck. If a fellow gets away well in the spring he takes it easily and hits well. If he gets away badly he begins to try to make himself hit safely. You can't do that, you know. When you begin to force your game, you are gone.

"I got off badly and I have hit in streaks. For two or three days I hit well. Then I have a two or three day slump. And so on. I get angry at myself sometimes and press my swing. That hurts. Withal, I have hit well enough to reach the .300 mark if I have just two weeks of good luck."[27]

The Browns finally found their stride. At the end of July, they had won ten games in a row. At last, all the players were playing up to their preseason billing, and the pitching staff had coalesced around the veteran Eddie Plank and David Davenport. Marsans found peace at the plate. He ran the bases and continued to field his position with few peers.

The winning streak continued—eleven, twelve, thirteen games in a row. The Browns climbed in the standings to just seven games out of first place. In the fourteenth game of the streak, the Browns faced the World Series winners, the Boston Red Sox. On the mound for Boston was a young pitcher named George Herman "Babe" Ruth. "The gigantic youngster who pitched for Boston"[28]

was not at his best. The Browns triumphed 6–1. Marsans was one
for four with a sacrifice hit.

Though they had won fourteen consecutive games, the
Browns were still three and a half games out of the first division—
i.e., the top half of the League. Philip Ball, the owner of the team,
made his men a promise. Each member of the team would receive
a fifty-dollar suit if the team could make it to the first division and
hold the place for three days. And he gave them an even bigger
incentive. The notice that went up in the clubhouse at Sportsman's Park on the 4th of August promised the team a $5,000 bonus
if they could reach first place in the American League "for a day,
or for fifteen or twenty minutes, perhaps between a double
header."

The Browns finally lost, 4–1 to Boston, ending their streak.
The highlight of the game for many was the fight between the
Browns third baseman, Jimmy Austin, and Red Sox catcher Chester
Thomas. Thomas outweighed Austin by thirty pounds, but it did
not stop the Brown from landing the first punch. When Austin
was suspended for the fight, Jones announced that he would
play the versatile Marsans at third base to fill the void. The Browns
won the first game with Marsans at third, 3–2 over the Washington Senators, and his performance earned him a second game on
the job.

In the last game of the series, Marsans shifted back to center
field where he made an eighth-inning play that may have saved
the game for the Browns. St. Louis was ahead 4–0, but Washington had loaded the bases with only one man out. The Washington batter sent a sharp line drive to center. Marsans read the ball
perfectly, sprinted fifty yards directly toward second base, and
made a diving catch before scrambling to his feet and making a
perfect throw to home plate, driving the Senators' runner back to
third and preserving the lead and the victory.

The Browns outfield was heralded as one of the primary fac-
tors in the team's rebirth. They comprehended Jones's intellectual approach to baseball and were employing it. Shifting for every
batter it appeared to be "easier for the Biblical camel to tango
through the eye of the Biblical needle than it is for a long hit to
seep through this defense...."

"We're doing things automatically, now that we know how,"
said manager Jones. "In the spring we were learning. We were
stiff, awkward, and shaky. We knew the weakness of batters,

but it was an effort to remember. Now we never think, we just do it."[29]

Unfortunately, Marsans again slumped badly at the plate. Through one stretch in early September, he was hitless in twenty at bats.[30] But he continued to contribute. On September 17th, he was largely responsible for the Browns's victory over Walter Johnson and the Senators. Marsans drew a walk and eventually scored. But his biggest contribution to the win came in the eighth inning when a Washington batter hit a long drive to center. Marsans turned and sprinted toward the outfield fence at the crack of the bat. The play seemed impossible to many of the eight thousand fans. Marsans lept, in full stride, and extended his bare right hand to meet the sharply hit ball as it sailed over his shoulder. Marsans's catch was called "one of the most remarkable catches ever witnessed on a local field,"[31] and "by consensus of opinion in the press box at least, the greatest play of the season."[32]

There are moments in each season, a small number of plays, which transcend the summer-long grinding of baseball's gears. These few moments are more than exceptional baseball plays, they are remarkable and unique feats of athleticism that remind us why we pay to watch these men perform. This catch was one of those moments, when the home crowd falls silent in uncertainty, as the opponent's hit flies through the air. When the incredible play is made, cheers erupt. Even then the spectators find themselves thinking twice to be sure the catch was made, and feeling awe in the face of the truly exceptional.

As rapidly as the Browns put together their threat to rise to the top of the American League, they returned to their early season form. Pitching was one problem, but offensive punch was missing from the lineup, in part due to Marsans's inability to hit consistently. They were involved in a remarkable sixty-five games in which victory was decided by one run. Thirty-five of those games were losses.

Marsans departed for Havana on the 29th of September, leaving early to be by his wife who had taken ill.[33] Marsans finished second in the American league in stolen bases with forty-six, behind Ty Cobb's sixty-eight. Marsans accomplished this hitting .254, versus Cobb's .371 average. If base stealing were calculated in the same way as batting average, the number of steals divided by the number of times the player reached first base, Marsans

would have had the second best average in the league, .251, behind
Ty Cobb's .289 average. Marsans was also sixth in the league scoring from first base, reaching home plate 27.9 percent of the time.
Ty Cobb led the league, scoring a remarkable 48.1 percent of the
time that he made it to first base.[34]

Despite these facts, one writer for the *Globe-Democrat* wrote,
"Center fielder Marsans had a bad year with the bat. Probably
Marsans's failure to hit up to the speed he displayed while a member of the Cincinnati club of the National League had more to do
with the failure of the Browns to finish higher than any other
thing."[35] Prior to being enjoined from playing baseball for most
of two seasons, Marsans had batted .302 in his time in the major
leagues. Since being permitted to play again, Marsans had batted
only .239.

The Browns finished in fifth place in the American League,
twelve games behind the Boston Red Sox.

10

Frustration

The Browns headed south for spring training on March 3, 1917. Marsans had not been heard from, nor had Earl Hamilton, another Brown who spent the winter playing baseball in Cuba. This year, however, Marsans was uncharacteristically punctual, arriving on March 8th, after a rough voyage from Havana to New Orleans.

In the first scrimmage, Marsans proved the benefit of playing baseball through the winter when he hit two singles and a double, stole a base, and scored a run. Marsans was bolstered by sentiments that produced stories like the one titled "Leading Base Runner Is Armando Marsans." The story opened "Armando Marsans was the best base runner on either the Browns or Cardinals last year as his forty-six stolen bases in seventy-two attempts show. The fleet Cuban hit in rather poor form the first month, but he played winning ball every minute."[1] The story went on to list the many highlights on the base paths, in the outfield, and even at the plate that made up Marsans's 1916 season. But even in the compliments there were derogatory comments. "'Brown Skin' is working hard with the hope of being a real slugger, entitling him to the occupation of one of the clean-up positions in the batting order."

In the Browns' and Cardinals' annual pre-season series, the Browns lost the first game in the bottom of the ninth inning, though Marsans played exceptionally in the outfield and went two for four with a double, batting in the sixth position. "Fielder Jones was so elated over the work of Armando Marsans in yesterday's game with the Cardinals that he almost forgot the defeat. It was a great day for the Cuban."[2]

Three days later, on April 6th, 1917, the United States entered World War I. The declaration of war appeared in virtually every newspaper in the country: "Whereas, the Congress of the United States, in the exercise of the constitutional authority vested in them, have resolved, by joint resolution of the Senate and House of Representatives bearing date this day, that a state of war between the United States and the Imperial German Government which has been thrust upon the United States is hereby, formally declared."

Ban Johnson ordered that all teams in the American League receive military instruction and offered a prize of five hundred dollars for the team judged to do the best military drilling exercises at mid-season.[3] An Army instructor from Fort Sam Houston, Texas, was assigned to the Browns to train the athletes in "military tactics."[4] In the Browns' first exhibition of their drilling skills before a game on April 9, their exhibition was "crude enough to be termed farcical."

> Unless it can be held that the intelligence of some of the players is far below the average, there can be no reasonable excuse offered for their unsoldierly conduct during the brief period of Saturday's performance.
> When Sergeant Wisener gave the command to assemble in column of squads, every player should have found his place quickly and stood at attention. Instead some of them had to shift around three or four times before they found their proper positions. The alignment was poor and there were two or three men who were unnecessarily tardy. Many of them who did "fall in" promptly committed a gross breach of discipline by twisting and turning and talking while they should have been standing at attention.[5]

Players and fans debated the importance of continuing the baseball season with the country at war. One player defended the completion of the season saying, "There has been a disposition among the ballplayers to chafe at the idea of playing ball with the nation at war, and thousands of their fellow citizens enlisting. I have heard a number of players say that they will quit the game and enlist within a few weeks, and I admire their patriotism. There is another thing to be considered, however. I, and every other professional ballplayer, am engaged in furnishing amusement to millions of people who need that amusement and relaxation. The tension all over the nation is intense and baseball is going to do much to relieve this condition and keep things running in a normal sort of way."[6]

Though their drilling skills left much to be desired, the Browns started the season well, reaching second place in the American League in early May with an 11–8 record.

In a game on May 16th, the Yankees catcher, Les Nunamaker, made a comment about Marsans's forebears while Marsans stood in the batter's box, most probably calling Marsans a "nigger." Marsans hit a double. When he came to bat in the fifth inning Marsans told Nunamaker what he thought of him. Nunamaker responded in kind. "Marsans was sputtering out a mixture of English and Spanish and was getting a good grip on his bat when Umpire Billy Evans stepped between them and ordered play resumed. They continued their argument, however, and when things began to look serious, Evans ordered both players out of the game."[7] The report suggests Marsans was pereparing to hit Nunamaker with his bat. It is not known whether this was the case or whether this was another example of the tendency to portray Latinos as violent. What is clear is that Marsans, at age twenty-nine, was no more prepared to ignore such comments than he was in New Britain when he was ejected for fighting with "Nig" Rufiage. Marsans, clearly, continued to harbor his own prejudices about race. If he had believed that those of African ancestry were his equals, he would not have been offended by Nunamaker's comment.

In this sentiment he was not alone. In late May, the St. Louis area became embroiled in a race riot. In East St. Louis, Illinois, black laborers had been brought to town as strikebreakers. An angry mob formed after a meeting at city hall, began destroying property. In the second night of riots, "a score of negroes were beaten, and a half dozen negro homes were sacked and burned...."[8] The Illinois National Guard was called out but the peace was short-lived. On July 3rd, mobs of whites targeted African-Americans. "Shot, clubbed to death, roasted alive amid ruins of their own homes..."— the death toll of African-Americans was estimated at one hundred.

The Browns encountered trouble on the field after their good start. Injuries began to slow their progress, their pitching became inconsistent, and inexplicably their defense began to falter. The Browns' fall was demoralizing and the players seemed uninspired, though one reporter pointed out that Marsans was one of the few players whose effort was beyond reproach.[9]

By mid–June, Marsans was mired in a batting slump. His average had fallen to .235 and by the beginning of July it was as low as .231. Jones's long-standing faith in his Cuban outfielder finally weakened and Marsans was benched during a game on June 9th.[10] Marsans lost his starting job in early July. He had reached the nadir of his career. "The Cuban ... has never been able to regain his National League hitting stride. His failure to hit grew on his nerves and a few weeks ago he came to the conclusion that St. Louis was his 'jinx' town. He asked Manager Jones to trade him believing that he could do himself and the club no good here."[11] Jones arranged a trade with the New York Yankees that sent Armando Marsans to New York in exchange for Lee Magee.

On July 17, 1917, Armando Marsans reported to the New York Yankees. The franchise that would win twenty-seven World Series in the 20th century had yet to begin its reign over baseball. New York City, the largest and most cosmopolitan urban center in the United States, gave the Yankees broad exposure. But it was the New York Giants in the National League who were the favorites of the city in the first decades of the century.

The Yankees and the Giants shared the Polo Grounds, located at 8th Avenue and 155th Street. The oddly shaped outfield measured a short 277 feet down the left field line and an even shorter 256 feet to the foul pole in right. But it was 433 feet to the wall in center field, 455 feet to the alley in left field and 449 to the alley in right centerfield. This expanse was one of the largest centerfields in all of baseball. The Yankees were hoping Marsans's speed in center field would shore up their defense.

The novelty of a Cuban in the major leagues had worn off in the years since 1911. There were now five Cubans, including Marshals, playing for teams in the National and American leagues, and one of them was playing for the Yankees when Marsans came to New York. Ángel Aragón had played with the Yankees in 1914 but lasted only six games before being demoted to the minor leagues, largely due to his inability to speak and understand English. Aragón took English classes while playing with the minor leagues and wrote to the Yankees manager frequently, displaying his improving language skills. He was brought back to the major leagues in 1916, though he played in only twelve games. In 1917 he was seeing sporadic play as a utility man for the Yankees. Aragón and Marsans were very different sorts of men. Aragón was said by a Cuban newspaper to be modest, humble, and a little neurotic. The same paper described Marsans as valiant, decided, admirable on defense, and audacious on the attack.[12]

Marsans played in the outfield as soon as he reported to the Yankees. The Cuban was three for nine in his first two games, scoring two runs. Marsans improved the Yankees outfield but the team continued its roller coaster ride, showing strong ability and potential in one game and then looking flat in the next.

It seemed Marsans was correct about St. Louis being a curse for him. Free from the hex, and playing on the biggest stage in baseball, Marsans shone. His charisma and his ability earned him a devoted following among the Yankee fans. In a fifteen game span in late July and early August, Marsans had sixteen hits in fifty-three at bats, totaling a .302 batting average for that period. He maintained his great defense and scored seven runs in those games.

On August 10, in a game in New York against Cleveland, the Yankees scored five runs in the first inning, the last driven in by Marsans's double. The Cuban advanced to third on a sacrifice fly. The next Yankee hit a fly ball to right field. Marsans went back to third base and put his foot on the bag, ready to tag up and head for home as soon as the ball was caught. Marsans watched the right fielder squeeze the ball in his glove and dashed for home, intending to slide on the foul-territory side of the plate to avoid the catcher's tag. He slid on his right hip, hooking his left leg back so that he would touch the plate with his left foot. Marsans beat the throw, but his metal spikes caught in the rubber of home plate. The momentum of the slide carried him forward, and his left leg snapped just above the ankle.

As the umpire signaled safe with his two arms, Marsans writhed in pain on the dirt. He was carried to the Yankees' clubhouse on a stretcher, attended to by the Polo Grounds doctors, and then transferred to the German Hospital.

Marsans's 1917 season was over.

Many fans visited Marsans in the hospital, including the Cuban consul. The monotony of a three-week convalescence in a pre-air-conditioning New York hospital in August must have been nearly unbearable. The doctors were pleased with the way the leg healed, and Marsans finally left the hospital and headed home, arriving in Havana, as he had in 1912, limping ashore.

11

New York

The New York Yankees' new manager for 1918 was Miller Huggins. Huggins had played and managed against Marsans for several years in the National League. As a result, Huggins knew well Marsans's ability on the diamond and was especially impressed by Marsans's ability to cover the outfield.[1]

The Yankees went to Macon, Georgia, for spring training. The camp began with Marsans's whereabouts unknown. While waiting for Marsans to join the team, Huggins tentatively set his outfield around the Cuban in centerfield. Huggins remained optimistic about Marsans's arrival, expecting him virtually every day. But after ten days, Marsans still had not arrived. The rumor going around camp was that Marsans, the only Yankee not to have reported, was en route from Cuba with Miguel González.[2] Huggins's reaction to Marsans's tardiness was less of anger and more of concern. The Yankees waited, ten days, then two weeks, hoping to find Marsans on a train from Jacksonville, Florida. "The silence and non-appearance of Marsans has Huggins perplexed." Huggins responded by ordering a Yankees scout to go to Cuba to locate Marsans, but the scout did not have a passport and could not make the trip.[3]

Marsans did not report because he was attending to his sick

mother. By not communicating with the Yankees, Marsans made the ground fertile for the rumors about his absence. Instead of investigating, the press reverted to viewing Marsans through stereotypes. "Marsans has not written or communicated with Huggins. It is likely, however, that he is holding out for more money. The Cuban does not verily appreciate the fact that [the owners of the Yankees] Messrs. Ruppert and Huston did him a big favor by purchasing him from the lowly Browns last year, and then paying his hospital bills when he broke his leg."[4]

The strength of stereotypes can often be seen in how they are able to dominate factual evidence that contradicts their premises. "Armando Marsans, the temperamental Castillian"[5] had never held out for more money, only in 1912 did he write Herrmann saying he felt he deserved more money but would not hold out for it if Herrmann were not of the same opinion.[6] As to the hospital bills, was it unreasonable for Marsans to expect the Yankees to pay his medical costs, which were a result of an injury Marsans suffered on the field, playing for the Yankees?

On April 24th, Marsans officially reported to the team in New York, having played for, and managed, the league-champion team that winter in Havana. It was the day of the Yankees' home opener. Marsans and everyone else in attendance witnessed "a patriotic demonstration of unusual impressiveness."[7] A sixty-piece band played the national anthem and "other stirring martial and patriotic airs."[8] Large contingents of uniformed men from the Army and Navy were in the Polo Grounds that day. Patriotic colors draped from the stadium, American flags flew from every pole and bunting hung throughout the park. Liberty Bond sales booths were installed near each dugout to raise money for the war effort. The players themselves sold bonds from the booths, aided by young women walking among the seated spectators. A total of $110,000 in bonds was sold to the small crowd of 10,000 that day.[9]

The United States was fully focused on the war and the 1918 season was shadowed with uncertainty. Many players had volunteered to fight in Europe while others faced the probability of being drafted. Organized baseball was tightening its belt in anticipation of a slowdown in attendance, which the opening day figures confirmed. Teams lowered many players' salaries. Players would have to handle their own luggage to and from the train depot and their home. *Per diems* were set at three dollars and a $1.25 allowance was made for meals taken on trains.

Unlike in the past, Marsans came north in 1918 out of shape. Presumably, taking care of his mother had left neither time nor energy to remain in condition to play baseball. It would be another ten days before Marsans got into his first game for the 1918 season.

Marsans's performance in that game "immediately sent the mercury up in Miller Huggins' thermometer of hope.... The showing the Cuban gave may win him a regular berth in the outfield at once."[10] Marsans was five for nine in the first two games. The Cuban press marveled about "Marsans's resurgence to life in baseball. When he seemed dead as a batter and when he himself ... seemed to have little confidence in his current condition, went to New York lacking confidence and fearful. Now, it turns out that his batting is sensational...."[11]

Marsans continued as the Yankees' regular centerfielder, his playing time assured by his rising batting average. Marsans hit .283 in his first thirteen games. A week later, he had raised his average to .290, 17th in the American League. Uncharacteristically, he only stole one base up to that point in the season. The Yankees, as a team, were leading the league in batting and perhaps Huggins was allowing his bats to advance runners instead of having them attempt steals. Another possible explanation was that Marsans was slower because of the broken leg he had suffered the previous season.

But Marsans had not yet earned a regular position in the outfield. He returned as a starter in center field in mid–June due to an injury to the other centerfielder. The Cuban went on a six-game hitting streak during which he batted .360. When the regular center fielder recovered from his injury, Marsans continued to play the position full time.

Marsans and the Yankees were battling the Boston Red Sox for first place in the American League and, as of June 7th, the Yankees were in second place—two games behind the Red Sox. In a game on the 13th in Cleveland, Marsans was again in center field. In the fourth inning of a tight game, an Indians batter hit a high fly ball to left center. "Ping" Bodie, the Yankees left fielder, and Marsans both went toward the ball. Bodie stopped to let Marsans catch it, but in a lack of communication the ball dropped between the players for a double. The two players argued in the outfield before returning to their positions. The error led to two runs for the Indians. Marsans and Bodie continued to argue on the bench as the Yankees came to bat. After exchanging heated words, the players went for each other but their teammates managed to restrain the two players.

On July 19th, the secretary of war declared that baseball was a "non-productive and non-essential"[12] industry and players between twenty-one and thirty-one, the ages covered by the draft, must shift into essential industry work or lose their deferred draft status. The ruling threw the remainder of the 1918 season into uncertainty. Of the three hundred and eighteen players in the National and American Leagues, two hundred and forty-seven were between the ages of twenty-one and thirty-one, and therefore would have been eligible for the draft.[13]

Organized baseball pledged its complete commitment to the service of its country and full compliance with the ruling. Many players quit their contracts after the order and took jobs in ship-building yards and steel plants that had baseball leagues so they could continue to play. Ban Johnson, president of the American League, declared that his league would end its season on the 22nd of July barring some change in events.

In the middle of this turmoil, Marsans received word that his mother had again fallen seriously ill. He went to his manager and explained the situation. Huggins, understanding the issue, gave Marsans permission to return to Cuba immediately, asking only that his outfielder return to the Yankees as soon as his mother's health improved. Marsans boarded the train for Key West that night and sailed to Havana, arriving in Cuba on July 19th.[14]

Reaction in the New York papers described a rupture between Marsans and Huggins and the Yankees. The stories said Marsans had taken offense at being benched and having his playing time limited. Marsans had been hitless in seventeen at bats in six games beginning on June 30th. His slump had landed him on the bench for the first game of a doubleheader against the White Sox. Marsans played the second game and got two hits in four at bats but his average had plummeted to .233.

The temperamental Marsans, according to the stories, left the Yankees without giving notification or explanation. The contrast between the facts and perceptions of the event again showed the tendency to revert to ingrained stereotypes about Latinos. But the pattern throughout Marsans's career shows that these stereotypes lay dormant while Marsans behaved in accordance with ideas of accepted behavior but quickly came to the fore when Marsans entered into conflict or his actions were in some way inexplicable.

The abbreviated 1918 regular season had been extended from July 22 to Labor Day and was followed by a World Series. The Yankees had faded rapidly in the American League race after Marsans's departure. Armando Marsans never returned to the Yankees and would never play major league baseball again. Approaching thirty-two years old, Marsans was certainly not the oldest man in baseball. Why then did Marsans not return to the major leagues? His absence from play in Cuba that winter, his first in fourteen seasons, suggests that his mother's illness may have extended through the fall. Marsans's love of baseball had not been extinguished. He did return to the Cuban diamond the following season but then did not participate in the subsequent year. It is probable that Marsans's eroding offensive output in the United States left him frustrated, and being a man of many interests, he decided to close the door on the chapter of his life that was his career in the United States while still participating in the game he loved in Cuba.

A Belated Return

On July 11, 1923, the *Louisville Times* announced Armando Marsans's return to baseball in the United States: "Armando Marsans, one of the best Cuban performers ever to pastime in baseball circles in this country and who performed brilliantly while a member of the Cincinnati Reds, has been engaged by the Colonels." Now thirty-five years old, Marsans had last played baseball in the United States with the Yankees in July of 1918.

The minor-league Louisville Colonels signed Marsans on the recommendation of their Cuban center fielder, Merito Acosta. Merito Acosta had played in the American League with Washington and Philadelphia for five seasons and had been in the minors since 1919. He broke his ankle playing early in the season, leaving the Colonels with a shortage of good outfielders. Acosta recommended Marsans to the Louisville management. The two Cubans had played against one another over the previous winter in Cuba and Acosta knew Marsans was still capable of contributing to the Colonels. Marsans, responding to an inquiry by the Louisville management, telegraphed that he was in good shape and ready to get into the game.

Marsans and Buck Herzog had had their first major confrontation in Louisville. It was there in 1914 that the injured

Marsans had swung one-handed in batting practice, and the conflict led directly to Marsans signing with the Federal League. In recounting the event, the *Louisville Post* reminded its readers that Marsans was "Latin and temperamental."[1]

It is not clear what motivated Marsans to return to organized baseball. Did he aspire to climb back into the major leagues, or was this one last adventure, an opportunity to prove to himself that he could still play in the United States, if only in a top minor league?

Marsans was a wealthy man. There was no pressing financial need for him to play. Marsans was not simply returning to organized baseball at the urging of his friend Acosta. He had wanted to reenter organized baseball earlier in 1923, attempting to sign a contract with the Ft. Worth team of the Texas League at the beginning of the season. But reportedly the Yankees, who still held a reserve claim on Marsans, refused to permit him to join the team.

Marsans arrived in Louisville from Havana and then joined the Louisville team in Minneapolis on July 14th. In his first game for the Colonels, Marsans played at first base. He handled the position well and without error but was hitless in five at bats. The Colonels then crossed the Mississippi for a series against St. Paul but Marsans did not play. In St. Paul, Marsans was reunited with his former Reds teammate, Miguel González. González had been demoted to the minors for the 1922 season after nine years in the majors. He would return to the National League in 1924 for another eight years, playing for St. Louis and the Chicago Cubs, for whom he appeared briefly in the 1929 World Series. González would become the first Latino to manage in the major leagues, serving as interim manager for the Cardinals in 1938 and again in 1940.

Marsans saw sporadic play with the Colonels as a substitute in the outfield and at first base. His opportunity came when the Colonels' rightfielder injured himself. Marsans played regularly in the outfielder's three-week absence. The Cuban fielded his position well but it took a few games for him to become comfortable at the plate.

"Marsans has been showing alert baseball ever since he joined the club. He pulled an unusual play yesterday when he advanced from first to second on a fly (to left field)…. The odds are against this play because the base runner is running into the throw. The runner must know how to vary his slide…. The Blues didn't expect the play yesterday, and Marsans wasn't hard pressed to get away with it."[2]

The Colonels were in third place in the American Association, with fifty-two wins and forty-six losses. Marsans became a vital part of the Louisville team. After one doubleheader, the *Louisville Times* called Marsans "the individual star of the two games." He also earned the title "King of the Association Bunters" with his deft handling of the bat.[3] The Cuban began to dominate American Association pitching. He had thirteen hits in thirty-six at bats and scored seven runs in a homestand in Louisville. Marsans's overall batting average was nearing .300, the second best on the Colonels. But the streak ended when Marsans sprained his wrist sliding into second base and was forced to watch the Colonels for several games seated on the bench.

One hundred miles up the Ohio River from Louisville, Kentucky, Marsans's former team, the Cincinnati Reds, was in the heat of a pennant race. By mid–July it was a three-team battle in the National League, with the Cincinnati Reds, the New York Giants, and the Pittsburgh Pirates locked in a struggle for the National League pennant.

One of the key players in the Reds' pennant dreams was the Cuban Adolfo Luque. The thirty-one-year-old Luque was known as "the pride of Havana." His light blue eyes and black hair, which he wore long, won a devoted following among young women; "Flocks of flappers try to waylay Dolf ... exactly as they prowl upon the trail of Rudolph Valentino."[4] He holds the distinction of being the first Latino to pitch in a World Series game, and the first Latino to win a World Series, pitching five innings of scoreless baseball in two games in the 1919 series against the Chicago White Sox.

By the middle of the 1923 season, Luque, despite an early-season lack of run support, was putting together one of the great seasons of any pitcher in modern baseball. "The short, catlike Cuban"[5] won his seventeenth game by the end of July, having suffered only three losses. Some believed he had a chance at Jack Chesbro's modern-day record of 41 victories in a season, set in 1904. Best of all, Luque was magical against the New York Giants. He had beaten the Giants three times in 1923 without a loss. He volunteered to pitch out of turn to face the Giants as many times as possible in the remaining twelve games against the Reds' main rival, saying, "A lucky pitcher should press his luck. Send me in four or five games of the twelve if my luck holds good."[6]

Adolfo Luque. The *Louisville Times* (July 14, 1923) reported that Giants
manager John McGraw named Luque the best pitcher in the major leagues
in the 1923 season. (National Baseball Hall of Fame Library, Cooperstown, N.Y.)

At the beginning of August, the Giants came to Cincinnati for a crucial series. The Giants were in first place in the National League with sixty-four wins and thirty-five losses. Cincinnati was close on their heels with a record of sixty-one and thirty-eight. Luque took the mound for the first game of the series. The Giants counted on a new tactic to help break the Reds' spell—they would rattle the Reds by verbally harassing them on the field. Their primary target was going to be Luque.

"Players on opposing teams, knowing him to be rather hot-headed, as is typical of the Latin races, 'ride' him a great deal."[7] The Giants demolished Luque and won the first game fourteen to four. The Reds also lost the second game against the Giants. Then they lost both games of a doubleheader. In front of six thousand fans, Luque took the mound for the desperate Reds in the fifth and final game of the series. He gave up two runs in the first inning but settled down, giving up only one more run in the next six innings. The Reds scored twice in the bottom of the seventh to make the score three to two. In the top of the eighth inning, Luque retired the first two Giants but then gave up four consecutive hits. The Giants began yelling "caustic comments" at the Cuban.[8]

With two runs in and men on first and third, the next Giant batter stepped to the plate. Luque's first pitch was high and inside, an intentionally wasted pitch designed to brush back the hitter and reestablish Luque's presence. More yells erupted from the Giants' bench in response.

Luque looked over at the Giants. He left the mound and walked slowly but deliberately toward the New York bench. As he crossed the foul line, Luque casually flipped the ball to the home plate umpire and kept walking toward the Giants' bench. Luque went directly to Casey Stengel, then a Giant outfielder, and threw a punch at him. Stengel ducked and the punch glanced off his shoulder. One of the Giants grabbed Luque and dragged him away. The Reds players sprinted from their positions in the field and the bench to help their pitcher.

Policemen ran over to the Giants' bench and tried to separate the players. They grabbed Luque and took him back to the Reds' dugout while the scuffle continued. Fans jumped onto the field and ran toward the jumble of players. The police managed to keep them back. Luque, after taking a drink of water, grabbed a bat and ran back toward the Giants' bench. The police stopped him before he could exact his revenge on Stengel. Both Luque and Stengel were ejected from the game and the Reds lost 6–2.

Luque had most probably heard one of the Giants call him a "nigger," but accounts differ as to who made the comment that so incensed the Cuban. "I was called a name that no man has to take, and I am positive that Stengel called it—I think I ought to know his voice by this time. I'm sorry for the row, but I could do nothing else."[9]

Several fans came into the clubhouse after the game claiming they had heard Stengel make the comment and were willing to sign affidavits to that effect. But John McGraw, the Giants' manager, insisted that Luque was mistaken. McGraw had been seated near Stengel on the bench, and claimed it had been Giants outfielder Billy Cunningham who made the remark that triggered Luque's fury.[10]

Luque had been involved in a similar incident when he was playing with the Louisville Colonels several years before. Luque attacked an opposing player who in "making a remark classifying Cubans with the black race, had used a term suggesting that his [Luque's] individual lineage was not all that could be desired."[11] Luque had also attacked an umpire, who admitted making a derogatory comment. Both Luque and the umpire were fined one hundred dollars.[12] Luque maintained he had "struck in what he considers the defense of his honor and the honor of the Cuban race."[13]

After the incident between the Reds and the Giants, John Heydler, president of the National League, suspended Luque indefinitely. "We are going to rally," responded Luque, "and it may be necessary to suspend some more of us before we can be downed and kept down ... I want to tell the world, right now, that this ball club is unjustly treated and that the umpires don't live up to the rules. All season long, other players have been permitted to call our men names and use vile language as they wish, and no check has been put upon them, but if a Red opens his mouth he is chased off the field—maybe suspended."[14]

Luque's suspension was lifted a week later, in time for a game against the Giants in New York. When Luque was introduced, the New York fans booed. He pitched well and also hit a home run to help his team to a 6–3 victory. Fearing action by the league, the Giants did not taunt Luque in this game and his performance and demeanor seemed to win over the New York crowd, who applauded his accomplishments.[15]

Luque won ten more games, finishing the season with twenty-seven wins and eight losses and a 1.93 earned run average. He led all major league pitchers in wins, earned run average, shutouts, and winning percentage. The Reds finished the 1923 season in second place, four and a half games behind the Giants.

For years after the incident, Luque's name and the memories of the fight were inseparable. The incident eclipsed Luque's remarkable season and would become highly significant for other Latinos who were playing, or would play, in the major leagues. Luque's act left an indelible image of the hot-tempered, potentially violent Latino in the minds of baseball fans. Unlike the misinterpretations of many of Marsans's actions, which incorrectly reinforced negative conceptions of Latinos, Luque's attack and its motivation were exactly in line with stereotypes of Latinos. There were no misinterpretations in this case; Luque was unable to control his temper and lashed out violently as a result. The event, however, tainted more than just Luque's name, for in reinforcing the stereotype of the temperamental Latino, Luque's punch assured that not only he, but all Latinos would be viewed as temperamental. When Ty Cobb went into the stands after fans taunting him, it was the act of a cantankerous man. When Luque was involved in violence on the field, he was not an individual but a representation of the Latino race, powerless against the grip of his volatile temper.

Back in Louisville, Marsans's reemergence and performance caught the eye of *The Sporting News*. His hitting earned praise but it was his mastery of the craft of base running that was the focus of the article. The story related how Marsans hit a "mean twister to a point back of third."[16] Marsans raced to first, having lost just a bit of his speed in the five years since he last played. The third baseman turned around and ran to the ball in shallow left field. He fielded the ball just as Marsans reached first base and wrongly assumed Marsans was stopping there. The Cuban did not hesitate in running to second base. He arrived there safely, having caught everyone off guard.

> The audacity of the thing startled players and spectators alike. Few had ever seen anything of the sort before, although it used to be worked occasionally by some of the old-timers. Marsans pulled the trick while in the big show, but he didn't pull it with any frequency. It is something that would be spoiled by frequent repetition, and Marsans is successful at it because he knows when to do it.... There is not a more intelligent player

in the game than Marsans, who seems to have an uncanny
knack of knowing what to do and when to do it.[17]

The reaction of the Louisville fans to Marsans's style of play
hints at stereotypes they may have had of Latinos:

> He (Marsans) is showing them how the old-timers used to run
> the bases in the major leagues. So new and startling have been
> the Cuban's stunts along the paths that comparatively few of
> the folks hereabouts have yet come to an appreciation of the
> worth of it. When Marsans negotiates a base or two or three,
> many of the spectators, unwilling to give full praise for really
> marvelous performance—a bad habit of Louisville bugs, by the
> way—withhold from the Senor the credit due him and ascribe
> it to bone-domed base running, blessed with good luck.[18]

Marsans was back from a wrist injury after a week on the bench.
Though his batting average was over .300, his playing time inexplicably began to shrink. He sat on the bench for most of the latter half
of August, appearing primarily as a pinch runner or pinch hitter.

The Colonels released Marsans at the beginning of September. The *Louisville Herald* printed the following on September 5,
"Marsans made a good impression upon Louisville fans. He was
not as fast on his feet as in his big league days, which was to be
expected. He hit Association pitching well, but the steady playing
of day in and day out was too much of a strain upon him."[19] It
would have been difficult to surmise what the effects of "steady
playing" would have been on Marsans because he did not have it
with the Colonels. Marsans played in 45 games as a Colonel and
batted an impressive .322. It is difficult, therefore, to give credence
to reports that his performance was the cause of the rupture.

"Like a Mystery Play, This Story Gives No Answer" was the title
of an article appearing in the September 13 issue of *Sporting News*.
It recounted all of the rumors about Marsans's departure circu-
lating in Louisville, ranging from management's inability to pay
the Cuban to Marsans's homesickness. The article also speculated
that one reason for Marsans's departure may have been "temperament, with which Armando has always been bountifully
blessed."[20] None of the theories was acceptable to the *Sporting News*.

The passing of time has not shed any light on Marsans's departure from Louisville. Perhaps he had received a better offer—from
New York.

13

The Other Side of Segregation

Baseball historians have classified the All Cubans team with which Marsans played in the summer of 1905 as a major black team. Though the All Cubans had no official affiliation with any organized group of African-American teams and their 1905 tour included games against white teams, the mixed racial make-up of the All Cubans has earned them a place in African-American baseball history.

There was no affiliation between black baseball teams in the first decade of the 20th century. Most teams barnstormed for the season, playing local teams, black or white, in a prolonged road trip. This meant it was easier for Marsans's stint with the racially mixed All Cubans to be overlooked by New Britain and the Cincinnati Reds. Had this information been made public it would have proven nothing about Marsans's heritage, but it would have branded him in the eyes of the white American public with a stigma that would have made it more difficult for him to play in the major leagues.

Marsans was probably not the first player to have played on a racially mixed squad and then play in the major leagues. Fellow

Cuban Pedro Dibut would follow in Marsans's path as a white
player who played with the Cuban Stars (West) and then later with
the Cincinnati Reds, but that was after Marsans's career in Cincinnati.[1] The concerns whites held about black ballplayers claiming
to be Latinos of purely Iberian descent were real and expressed
in the scouting report on Almeida sent to the Cincinnati Reds in
1911. This makes Marsans's rise to the major leagues from a team
composed in part of Afro-Cubans unusual.

What Armando Marsans did after leaving the Louisville
Colonels in the late summer of 1923 was more unusual. He joined
a baseball team in New York that was a member of an African-
American league. The loose constellation of early 20th century
African-American teams had solidified in 1920 with the formation
of the eight-team Negro National League. In 1923 they were joined
by the Mutual Association of Eastern Colored Baseball Clubs, better known as the Eastern Colored League. Each league had a team
named the Cuban Stars for the 1923 season. Historians distinguish
the two teams with a geographical denotation. The Cuban Stars
based in Cincinnati and playing in the Negro National League are
referred to as Cuban Stars (West). The New York team with which
Marsans played is called the Cuban Stars (East).

New York in 1923 was at the height of the Jazz Age and
Harlem, where the Cuban Stars played, was in its renaissance.

On Sunday, April 29th, the Eastern Colored League season
opened at the Protectory Oval. African-American and white spectators attended the game in equal numbers. The Cuban Stars team
featured outfielders Alejandro "El Caballero" Oms, and Pablo
Mesa. José Fernández was the catcher, Bartolo Portuondo played
third base, Pelayo Chacon was the shortstop, and Perez was at first.
A young, tall Cuban named Martin Dihigo, who would come to be
known as "El Inmortal," played second base and would develop
into one of the greatest players of any color in baseball history.
Oscar was a talented spitballer, and Fabre, Vidal Lopez, and Juanelo
Mirabel joined him on the pitching staff. There was no doubt about
the dominant heritage of the many of the Cubans Stars; their dark
skin forbade them from ever crossing over to the major leagues.

The owner of the Cuban Stars (East), Alejandro Pompez, was
a mulatto from Key West. Pompez lived a flashy life. He was said
to have ties to the mob, and would flee the United States after an
indictment by a special prosecutor in 1936. Though a shady figure,
Pompez won the trust of his players.[2]

By early July, the Cuban Stars were in second place in the six-team Eastern Colored League. They gained ground on the Philadelphia-based Hilldale team and by August 4th, their record was 17–10 compared to Hilldale's 23–12. The Cuban Stars took first place a few days later before leaving for the rest of August to play games in Massachusetts against teams outside the league.

By the time the Cuban Stars returned to New York from Massachusetts, Marsans had been convinced to join the team. Marsans's decision to play in the Negro Leagues provides an interesting comparison of the views of race relations in Cuba and the United States. Unlike the rigidly segregated world of baseball in the United States, Cubans of all races had been playing professional baseball on the same teams since soon after the turn of the century. Marsans had come of age in this cosmopolitan baseball system. Marsans was familiar, if not friendly, with many of the players on the Cuban Stars team, having played with or against nearly all of them in the Cuban League during the winter. Cubans were able, if for only nine-innings, to put aside preconceptions and allow baseball to exist as a meritocracy; between the lines of the diamond, a man was judged not by his appearance, but by his physical ability and his understanding of the game.

Marsans, however, was a product of a culture, like that of the United States, in which blacks were viewed as being unequal to whites. He had absorbed these values as evidenced by his strong reactions to being called a "nigger" in New Britain in 1909. Judging by his reaction, Marsans probably did not feel that blacks were his equals off the field, but on the field, Marsans reveled in the game and it seems that the color of his teammates or his opponents did not matter.

There is little information available about Marsans's time with the Cuban Stars. How he felt about his brief tenure on the team and why he did not return after the 1923 season will not, one hopes, remain unanswered questions.

14

A Pioneer to the End

Manager John McGraw of the New York Giants had always been a fan of Armando Marsans. He had watched Marsans play many games as a Cincinnati Red and realized Marsans had an intuitive sense of baseball and understood when to break free of the accepted ways of playing the game. When Marsans jumped to the Federal League, McGraw tried to orchestrate a trade that would bring Marsans to the Giants' outfield. Nine years later, McGraw spent part of the 1923-1924 off-season in Cuba and convinced Marsans to come north with the Giants, as a coach. Marsans, now thirty-six years old, accepted McGraw's offer and joined the Giants at their spring training camp in Sarasota, Florida.

Toward the end of the training camp, McGraw received word that the Elmira, New York, franchise in the Class A New York–Pennsylvania League was looking for a manager. McGraw wired one of the Elmira officials, "Capable manager and catcher is available for use in Elmira. John McGraw." Who is to blame for the grammatical error is not clear. But the use of "is" instead of "are" in the telegram left the Elmira franchise believing they could acquire a catcher who was a player-manager.[1]

In 1924, Elmira, New York, had a population of fifty thousand. The town, located in central upstate New York, saw a baseball

163

franchise as a way to bring recognition to their community. After the financial backers of the 1923 team withdrew their support, the city of Elmira decided to reform the team. The new management sent telegrams around organized baseball, including to major league teams in spring training, asking for players to fill their roster.

When Elmira telegrammed McGraw asking for more details, he informed them he was offering Armando Marsans along with a catcher in the Giants' training camp. Elmira accepted. The local paper announced the signing of the new manager saying, "Marsans is well known in the baseball world. He was formerly an outfielder with the Cincinnati Reds and has acted as coach in the Giant training camp. His ability as a manager is unquestioned. Marsans is a Cuban."[2] No mention was made of the fact that Marsans had spent part of the previous season playing for a team in the Negro Leagues.

On the evening of April 3, 1924, Marsans arrived in Elmira as a pioneer in baseball in the United States—the first Latino manager of a team in organized baseball.

Over the next few days he met with the management of the Elmira team and together they laid out plans for the season. The top priority was the need to find the best players possible to wear the Elmira uniform for the rapidly approaching opening day.

Elmira ordered players to report for the first practice on April 15. On that cold, blustery day, Marsans led the team in exercises. Dunn Field was constructed like so many other minor league fields around the country: A grandstand, with a roof supported by view-obstructing girders, cradled the infield. There was a flagpole inside the fence in centerfield and colorful advertisements and a manually operated scoreboard on the outfield fence.

After that first practice observers in Elmira were optimistic:

> The players who worked out Monday, under the supervision of Manager Armando Marsans, appeared to have plenty of stuff as they cavorted about the field and sent the ball crashing against the fences during batting practice. But the most outstanding feature of the whole practice was Marsans himself. It took the Cuban manager just about three minutes to instill the idea into the squad that he was boss, and that they were going to do as he said, if they played at all. It was plain to see that the players were duly impressed. According to our way of thinking Marsans is the ideal manager. There will be no discouragement, no pessimism.

The fighting spirit will be instilled and if the team doesn't go
out and win ball games it won't be the fault of Armando
Marsans. That is very plain to be seen already.[3]

Elmira dominated its opponents in a series of pre-season exhibition games, with scores of 19–0, 10–0, and 26–5 against a variety
of local and visiting teams. Encouraged by these victories against
overmatched opponents, the local sportswriters picked Elmira as
a pennant contender.

On opening day, the Elks band headed a parade that made
its way from City Hall, through the town of Elmira, to Dunn Field.
The team followed the band and a long line of cars followed the
uniformed players. Marsans's nine had been named the "Colonels." They entered the stadium on opening day wearing baggy
white pin-striped uniforms with a cursive "E" on the left breast. A
week earlier, another Cuban had joined the team, when Marsans
arranged for first baseman Manuel Parrado to come to Elmira
from the Louisville Colonels franchise.

The team arrived at Dunn Field and the fans took their seats
to watch them warm up. The Colonels and their opponents from
Williamsport, Pennsylvania, marched to centerfield and stood by
the flagpole for the flag raising ceremony, then took batting practice before the mayor of Elmira threw the ceremonial first pitch.
The Elmira Colonels won the season opener 3–0 against the
defending league champions.

In rising to the top of the league, the Elmira team led by
Marsans proved the pre-season predictions correct. Marsans seemed
ageless. In centerfield, his defense was outstanding, and at the
plate, after a slow start, he began to hit well.

Manuel Parrado was also earning a place in hearts of Elmira's
fans. After his two-out, ninth-inning single scored the winning run
one writer said, "Parrado is a great fielder. He is going to be a
great hitter. He is on his way to the major leagues just as sure as
any player performing in the minors today is on his way to the big
show.... He is one of the most valuable men on the Colonel roster. No doubt of it."[1]

Reports in the Elmira paper covering Marsans and Parrado
were free of disparaging remarks about the players' ethnicity and
nationality. They were frequently identified as "Cuban," but the
paper did not use monikers for either player referring to their
culture or its language.

Political unrest in Cuba at the beginning of May presented opportunity for stereotypes of Cubans to resurface in the press's coverage of the events. What had begun as a small revolutionary movement in Cuba's Santa Clara province had spread to the adjoining Oriente province. Simultaneously, in response to a strike by stevedores, the government of the city of Havana declared martial law. The work stoppage spread to the streetcar workers, the taxi drivers, and then the bakers' union. The events were front-page news, but the Elmira paper covered them without derogatory judgment of Cubans or their political system.

On June 3rd, Colonels started a series against York, Pennsylvania, at Dunn Field. Their record of sixteen wins and seven losses placed them just behind the league-leading Scranton team.

York took a 1–0 lead in the second inning, but Elmira countered with a run in their half of the second, and took the lead with two more runs in the third. In the fourth inning, Marsans reached first base on a single. He broke for second base, but the York catcher threw him out attempting to steal.

After being called out, Marsans heard one of the York players yell an unspecified epithet at him. Marsans returned to the Elmira dugout. At the end of the half inning he walked over to the York bench, followed by several teammates, and demanded an explanation for the remark. The fans poured out of the bleachers and grandstand and onto the field, swarming around the York bench. "A free for all fight, which seemed imminent was averted when local officials took a hand in the matter and sent the players back to their respective dugouts."[5]

It is not clear what the epithet was. It may be surmised by Marsans's reaction, and the condemnation in the newspaper for the remark, that Marsans was again called the worst names for someone of African descent. The incident ended without conflict, in contrast to similar events in Marsans's youth.

Marsans's ability as a manager was heralded during the Colonels' early-season success. His performance on the field, which included a batting average that would top .300, and strong play in the outfield, showed he was still capable of making a contribution to a team. "There isn't a harder worker on the team than Marsans. He plays the game with his whole heart and soul and overlooks nothing that might bring about victory."[6] Presumably Marsans's management style could be summed up in a similar manner.

Both Cuban players received mention in a *Sporting News* article of June 12 titled "Marsans Makes Good as Pilot." Of Parrado the article said:

> Parrado is without question the greatest fielder of the local league. As a first baseman he is far superior to many performing in many higher leagues today. The only thing keeping him out of the big show is his hitting. He isn't a sure hitter, but is improving greatly in this respect. Parrado is unable to speak English, Marsans being the only member of the team who can understand him.[7]

Manuel Parrado, batting only .195 at the time of the *Sporting News* article, went on a hitting streak that raised his average to .282.

Elmira dropped to third place in the league by mid–June, with an 18–10 record. The Colonels continued to slide in the standings, and when the Colonels fell to fourth place, the *Elmira Advertiser* said:

> We predicted great things for the Colonels during the first part of the season. Their playing seemed to deserve it. But just now a shake-up seems to be the most logical way out of a bad situation. Certainly there are some players on the Colonels roster who are no benefit to the team. True, several members of the team are first class, conscientious players. Others may have the ability but they certainly are not showing it to any great extent. Drastic action seems necessary if Elmira is to have a winning aggregation.[8]

Mortimer Sullivan, president of the team, stated he had long felt there was a problem in the infield. But the president of the team also said, "It isn't good policy to sign many new players when you have a 15 player limit. You are more apt to disrupt the team than to make an improvement."[9] Counter to the president's statement, the team acquired four new players to try and shore up the team in mid–July, but the Colonels continued to lose. Elmira sank to sixth place in the league, with a 31–36 record. The contradiction between Sullivan's statement and action were indicative of the power struggle going on behind the scenes between Marsans and the Elmira management. Marsans was not someone who would tolerate a player not performing to his potential and believed that the team should have dropped those players. The Colonels did acquire four new players but Marsans was not given much time to integrate them into the team. President Sullivan announced, before a Sunday game against Harrisburg at Dunn Field, that Armando Marsans had submitted his resignation to the board of directors late the previous night and that they had accepted it immediately.

Prior to leaving for New York City on Monday afternoon, Marsans submitted the following letter to the *Elmira Advertiser*, which appeared in the July 27th edition:

> ...The reorganization I attempted here was but half successful because the owners of the Elmira Club failed to get the men needed to produce a winning team. I would not stay in Elmira and continue to lose games when it was easily possible to win by releasing men not producing and replacing them with available players who would produce.
>
> Even after the shake-up of last week some of the men on the team refused to work and produce as they should and when their owners declined to replace them at my request, thus giving every prospect of continued losses, there was nothing left for me to do but to express my disapproval in the form of my resignation.
>
> Parrado assures me that he will remain in Elmira at least for the immediate future. If my resignation failed to awaken club owners to the need for drastic action and better co-operation Elmira will not occupy the position it is rightfully entitled to. I am indeed proud of the loyal support of the local fans who have accorded me the whole-hearted co-operation during the few months I have remained in the city.[10]

Marsans's open letter was followed by a letter from Colonels President Sullivan, which read in part:

> To the Sporting Editor Elmira Advertiser:-
> Our attention has been called to a statement purporting to have been made by Marsans, formerly our baseball manager. This statement is full of errors. Marsans speaks of attempting a reorganization of the Elmira baseball club. From the time he reported until he departed he was helpless in the matter of getting players. Every player on the team was secured by the officers. We delivered to him a team that started out well but was unable to continue as a winner. When the time arrived that replacements seemed necessary Marsans could do nothing and again looked to the officials who secured Evers, McGregor, Moore, Walsh and O'Brien. With the new combination, Marsans again failed and he was dismissed as manager. He did not resign, but after he was told he was through, he requested permission to make such an announcement. We granted it, but his showing of ingratitude now impels us to state the truth. A

manager is supposed to assemble a team and direct its play. He did nothing toward assembling the team but left the task to us....

NO, MARSANS DID NOT RESIGN. HE WAS DISMISSED BECAUSE HE FAILED.
Dated Elmira, N.Y., July 30, 1924
OFFICIALS OF THE ELMIRA BASEBALL CLUB,
MORTIMER L. SULLIVAN,
President[11]

Notably, throughout the confrontation between Marsans and the Elmira management the Elmira newspaper never resorted to referring to Marsans's ethnicity as an explanation for any of his actions.

Marsans returned to Cuba where he appeared in only thirty-four games over the next four seasons. Marsans's dedication to the game, though, did not end with his last game in 1928. He continued to manage in Cuba and also in the Mexican League where he won championships in 1945 and 1946.

Armando Marsans died on September 3, 1960, in Havana, Cuba, one month short of his seventy-third birthday.

15

Game Called

In a poorly lit corner of Havana's Estadio Latinoamericano, a marble plaque hangs on a wall. Chiseled in the marble is a tribute to the greatest figures in Cuban baseball that reads:

Cuban Professional Baseball Hall of Fame
List of players that have been selected as
BASEBALL IMMORTALS
And have deserved this just recognition for their distinguished work
maintaining an undying memory of what they were in this
sport

Reading down the list of names that follow, one can visually trace Cuba's recent history. The inscription and the first column of names are flawlessly carved in the marble, the names lined with gold leaf. Farther down the list, the names are still beautifully worked, but they are no longer lined in gold. This change coincides with the Cuban Revolution. A decision presumably was made that the luxury of gold leaf could no longer be afforded. Still farther down the list, the beautiful craftsmanship vanishes and the names are crudely chiseled into the plaque. Years after the Revolution, the skilled craftsmen who once chiseled the names into marble were no longer alive and their craft had died with them.

171

The fifth name on the plaque is Armando Marsans. Like the craft of stone carving, Armando Marsans's story has been sacrificed to the Cuban Revolution. Forty years of Cuban communism have severed many of the ties with pre-revolution baseball, depriving two generations of much of the rich history of early Cuban players and teams.

Today, Havana's devoted baseball fans gather in the Parque Central to argue and discuss baseball each day. On an afternoon in April 1998, only one man responded when asked if he knew who Armando Marsans was. The man was at least seventy years old and could recall the Boston Red Sox 1941 lineup name for name. As he told me what little he knew about the man who was once perhaps his country's most famous citizen, several young men gathered around and listened in a reverent silence.

Though the oral and written baseball tradition has been unbroken in the United States, Marsans is also a forgotten figure here. His success and his popularity with fans did not prevent him from drifting into the dark corners of baseball history, yet his impact is still with us. His ability and success with the Cincinnati Reds in 1911, and also in 1912 and 1913, forced major league executives to realize that Latinos, especially Cubans, were capable of playing well at the major league level. The number of Cubans signed in 1912, 1913, and 1914 attests to this fact.

Jackie Robinson's 1947 signing with the Brooklyn Dodgers opened the floodgates to a large reservoir of African-American players talented enough to play in the major leagues. The beginning of the influx of Latino players was not as dramatic as the 1947 breaking of the color barrier, but today, reading the rosters of the major league teams, it is clear that the change was tectonic, not only in pace but also in scale.

The impact of Marsans's career goes beyond baseball. His career in American baseball influenced the collective unconscious of the United States. In the early 20th century, baseball was the dominant passion of the sporting public to a degree that is difficult to imagine today. Marsans was the first foreign-born Latino sports star our society knew, and one of America's first Latino celebrities. His fame challenged American preconceptions of Latinos by presenting the public with a Latino individual who did not always coincide with sterotyped ethnic characteristics. But, in the end, Marsans's challenge was unsuccessful.

Our country's feelings of superiority so greatly influenced our perceptions of other peoples that no person in Marsans's era was capable of changing those views. Marsans, and other early Latino players who faced these preconceptions and biases, were not only unable to change them for the better, but, usually unwittingly, reinforced them through their own actions.

Marsans's argument with Herzog, and his subsequent jump to the Federal League, exemplifies this dynamic. Adolfo Luque, walking into the New York Giants's dugout in 1923 and throwing a punch at Casey Stengel, continued this trend. As did Juan Marichal hitting John Roseboro with a bat, and more recently, Roberto Alomar spitting in umpire John Hirschbeck's face.

Many non–Latino fans saw these events as verification of the predominant stereotypes of Latinos, while forgetting that the history of baseball is dotted by outbursts of violence. The participants in this violence were only occasionally Latinos. When a white player committed an act of violence on the field, his ethnicity was not mentioned. Instead, the act was usually attributed to the pressures of the heat of battle, or to the individual's character.

Are there cultural differences between the United States and Latin American countries? Of course there are. In the western European tradition, emotions are generally suppressed, while in Latino culture the expression of feelings is prominent and accepted. These cultural differences were frequently manifest in Marsans's actions on and off the field.

"Our tendency," wrote Franz Boas, "to evaluate an individual according to the picture that we form of the class to which we assign him ... is a survival of primitive forms of thought. The characteristics of the members of the class are highly variable and the type we construct from the most frequent characteristics supposed to belong to the class is never more than an abstraction hardly ever realized in a single individual, often not even a result of observation, but an often heard tradition that determines our judgment. Freedom of judgment can be attained only when we learn to estimate an individual according to his own ability and character."[1]

Perhaps the most physically gifted of the early Cuban players, Marsans's exceptional athleticism complemented an innate understanding of the game's intricacies, acknowledged to be unequaled among his countrymen, and matched by only a handful of the best players in professional baseball. Armando Marsans was born to play baseball. But it is impossible to resist the temptation to see his career as star-crossed tragedy. How else can his story be explained? As a young man, Marsans rose through the ranks of baseball to make himself a star. But fate deprived him of baseball for two years, then allowed him to return to play with eroded skills. What could Marsans have achieved in a career uninterrupted by a two-year legal case? One of the great pursuits of baseball fans is to lament careers cut short, or talents diminished by injuries, and to speculate about what *might have been*.

Chapter Notes

Preface

1. Giamatti.

1. Homecoming

1. *Cincinnati Post*, July 16, 1912.
2. *La Lucha*, Havana, October 18, 1912.
3. González, p. 87.
4. González, p. 507.
5. Perez, p. 505.
6. Suarez discussion.
7. González, p. 77.
8. Bisbort, 1997 Library of Congress Calendar.
9. González, p. 104.
10. González, p. 118.
11. González, p. 123.
12. González, p. 123.
13. *Stamford Daily Advocate*, May 22, 1905.
14. *Stamford Daily Advocate*, May 22, 1905.
15. *La Lucha*, Havana, September 21, 1905.

2. Foreigners in a Foreign Land

1. *La Lucha*, December 2, 1906.
2. *Cincinnati Times-Star*, August 22, 1911.
3. National Commission 4th Annual Report 1908 case 286.
4. *Springfield Union*, June 16, 1911.
5. *Holyoke Daily Transcript*, April 25, 1907.
6. *New Britain Herald*, April 4, 1908.
7. *Sporting Life*, March 6, 1908.
8. *New Britain Record*, April 6, 1908.
9. *New Britain Herald*, April 9, 1908.
10. *New Britain Record*, April 6, 1908.
11. *Springfield Union*, April 26, 1908.
12. *New Britain Herald*, April 23, 1908.
13. *New Britian Record*, April 20, 1908.
14. *New Britain Herald*, April 30, 1908.
15. Peterson, p. 18.
16. Peterson, p. 25.
17. Peterson, p. 31.
18. Peterson, p. 29.
19. Peterson, p. 36.
20. *Springfield Union*, April 26, 1908.
21. *New Britain Herald*, June 26, 1908.
22. *New Britain Herald*, May 28, 1908.
23. *Sporting Life*, May 23, 1908.
24. *Sporting Life*, May 22, 1908.
25. *Springfield Union*, June 2, 1908.

26. *New Britain Herald*, May 4, 1908.
27. *Springfield Union*, July 1, 1908.
28. *New Britain Herald*, July 31, 1908.
29. *Springfield Union*, June 14, 1908.
30. *New Britian Herald*, July 7, 1908.
31. *New Britain Record*, July 8, 1908.
32. *Springfield Union*, July 8, 1908.
33. *New Britain Record*, July 6, 1908.
34. *New Britain Herald*, July 17, 1908.
35. *New Britain Herald*, July 20, 1908.
36. *New Britain Herald*, July 20, 1908.
37. *New Britain Herald*, August 11, 1908.
38. *New Britain Record*, August 26, 1908.
39. *Springfield Union*, July 24, 1909.
40. *Sporting Life*, March 6, 1909.
41. *New Britain Herald*, March 13, 1909.
42. *New Britain Record*, April 14, 1909.
43. *New Britain Herald*, March 30, 1909.
44. *New Britain Herald*, March 26, 1909.
45. *New Britain Record*, April 28, 1909.
46. *New Britain Record*, May 5, 1909.
47. *New Britain Record*, May 3, 1909.
48. *Springfield Union*, May 17, 1909.
49. *New Britain Record*, May 10, 1909.
50. *Springfield Union*, May 11, 1909.
51. *New Britain Herald*, May 12, 1909.
52. *Springfield Union*, May 19, 1909.
53. "Some Inside facts on Cuban Players in America," undated, Marsans file, Baseball Hall of Fame.
54. *New Britain Record*, May 14, 1909.
55. *Springfield Union*, May 19, 1909.
56. *Springfield Union*, July 24, 1909.
57. *New Britain Herald*, June 2, 1909.
58. *Springfield Union*, July 29, 1909.
59. *New Britain Herald*, July, 27, 1909.
60. *Springfield Union*, July 30, 1909.
61. *Springfield Union*, August 1, 1909.
62. *Springfield Union*, September 13, 1909.
63. *New Britain Record*, August 4, 1909.
64. *New Britain Record*, August 4, 1909.
65. *New Britain Herald*, April 30, 1910.
66. *New Britain Herald*, April 27, 1910.
67. *Springfield Union*, April 12, 1910.
68. *New Britain Herald*, May 20, 1910.
69. *Springfield Union*, April 30, 1910.
70. *Springfield Union*, May 20, 1910.
71. *New Britain Herald*, April 12, 1910.
72. *New Britain Herald*, June 1, 1910.
73. *Springfield Union*, May 25, 1910.
74. *Springfield Union*, July 23, 1910.
75. *New Britain Herald*, July 13, 1910.

76. *New Britain Herald*, July 23, 1910.
77. *Springfield Union*, August 13, 1910.
78. *New Britain Record*, April 13, 1911.
79. *New Britain Herald*, May 11, 1911.
80. *New Britain Herald*, May 12, 1911.
81. *New Britain Herald*, March 30, 1911.
82. *Springfield Union*, May 15, 1911.
83. *Springfield Union*, June 29, 1911.
84. *New Britain Herald*, May 12, 1911.
85. *New Britain Herald*, May 16, 1911.
86. *New Britain Record*, May 5, 1911.
87. *New Britain Record*, May 17, 1911.
88. *New Britain Herald*, May 17, 1911.
89. *New Britain Record*, May 17, 1911.
90. *New Britain Herald*, June 15, 1911.
91. *Springfield Union*, June 16, 1911.
92. *New Britain Record*, June 29, 1911.
93. *New Britain Herald*, June 27, 1911.
94. *New Britain Record*, June 29, 1911.
95. *Cincinnati Tribune*, June 23, 1911.

3. Opportunity

1. *Cincinnati Times-Star*, June 29, 1911.
2. Jacobson, p. 48.
3. Jacobson, p. 223.
4. Jacobson, p. 48.
5. Grant, p. 17.
6. Report on Almeida from Heilbroner, Almeida File, Baseball Hall of Fame.
7. Baseball Hall of Fame, Herrman Papers, Letter from Heilbroner, January 4, 1911.
8. Gonzalez, p. 45.
9. Grant, p. 29.
10. Grant, p. 193.
11. Grant, p. 53.
12. *Cincinnati Tribune*, July 30, 1911.
13. *Cincinnati Enquirer*, June 23, 1911.
14. *Cincinnati Enquirer*, July 1, 1911.
15. *Cincinnati Post*, June 20, 1911.
16. *Sporting News*, June 22, 1911.
17. *Cincinnati Times-Star*, June 22, 1911.
18. *Cincinnati Post*, July 13, 1911.
19. "Interview with Chief Meyers," Meyers Clippings File, Baseball Hall of Fame.
20. *Cincinnati Times-Star*, June 30, 1911.
21. *Cincinnati Tribune*, June 31, 1911.
22. Baseball Hall of Fame, Herrmann papers, Letter.
23. *Cincinnati Enquirer*, July 19, 1911.
24. *New York Times*, July 20, 1911.
25. *Cincinnati Enquirer*, July 27, 1911.

26. *Cincinnati Times-Star,* July 11, 1911.
27. *Cincinnati Times-Star,* August 26, 1911.
28. *Cincinnati Times-Star,* July 15, 1911.
29. *Cincinnati Times-Star,* August 24, 1911.
30. *Cincinnati Times-Star,* October 9, 1911.
31. *Cincinnati Enquirer,* July 28, 1911.
32. *Cincinnati Enquirer,* July 16, 1911.
33. *Cincinnati Enquirer,* September 22, 1911.
34. *Cincinnati Times-Star,* September 13, 1911.
35. *Sporting News,* August 3, 1911.
36. *Cincinnati Times-Star,* September 20, 1911.
37. *Cincinnati Tribune,* August 31, 1911.
38. *Cincinnati Times-Star,* August 22, 1911.
39. *Cincinnati Tribune,* August 31, 1911.

4. Opportunity Seized

1. Baseball Hall of Fame, Letter, Herrmann papers.
2. Baseball Hall of Fame, Letter, Herrmann papers.
3. *Cincinnati Enquirer,* February 18, 1912.
4. *Cincinnati Times-Star,* June 25, 1912.
5. *Cincinnati Tribune,* February 28, 1912.
6. *Cincinnati Enquirer,* March 12, 1912.
7. *Cincinnati Tribune,* April 12, 1912.
8. *Cincinnati Enquirer* April 9, 1912.
9. *Cincinnati Times-Star,* April 3, 1912.
10. *Cincinnati Times-Star,* April 10, 1912.
11. *Cincinnati Times-Star,* April 11, 1912.
12. Gersham, p.107.
13. *Cincinnati Times-Star,* September 13, 1911.
14. *Cincinnati Tribune,* April 7, 1912.
15. *Cincinnati Enquirer,* March 19, 1912.
16. *Cincinnati Tribune,* April 12, 1912.
17. *Cincinnati Times-Star,* April 20, 1912.
18. *Cincinnati Times-Star,* May 1, 1912.
19. *Cincinnati Tribune,* May 4, 1912.
20. *Cincinnati Tribune,* May 8, 1912.
21. *Cincinnati Times-Star,* May 7, 1912.
22. *Cincinnati Tribune,* May 19, 1912.
23. *Cincinnati Times-Star,* April 25, 1912.
24. *Cincinnati Enquirer,* May 21, 1912.
25. *Cincinnati Tribune,* June 18, 1912.
26. *Cincinnati Enquirer,* May 26, 1912.
27. *Cincinnati Enquirer,* June 16, 1912.
28. *Cincinnati Tribune,* June 28, 1912.

29. *Cincinnati Times-Star,* June 1, 1912.
30. *Cincinnati Post,* July 16, 1912.
31. *Cincinnati Times-Star,* July 13, 1912.
32. *Cincinnati Times-Star,* June 27, 1912.
33. *Cincinnati Times-Star,* June 17, 1912.
34. *Cincinnati Enquirer,* June 18, 1912.
35. *Cincinnati Enquirer,* September, 3, 1912.
36. *Cincinnati Times-Star,* July 30, 1912.
37. *Cincinnati Enquirer,* July 28, 1912.
38. *Sporting Life,* August 3, 1912.
39. *Cincinnati Post,* July 26, 1912.
40. *Cincinnati Times-Star,* August 2, 1912.
41. *Cincinnati Times-Star,* August 5, 1912.
42. *Cincinnati Times-Star,* August 27, 1912.
43. *Cincinnati Times-Star,* May 24, 1912.
44. *Cincinnati Tribune,* August 16, 1912.
45. *La Lucha,* September 10, 1912.
46. *Cincinnati Times-Star,* May 23, 1913.

5. 1913

1. Marsans letter to Herrmann, January 5, 1913, Herrmann Papers, Baseball Hall of Fame.
2. Hermann letter to Marsans, January 13, 1912, Herrmann Papers, Baseball Hall of Fame.
3. Letter to Flanner, September 8, 1911.
4. *Cincinnati Post,* March 21, 1913.
5. Marsan letter to Herrmann, March 2, 1913, Marsans clippings file, Baseball Hall of Fame.
6. *Cincinnati Post,* March 7, 1913.
7. Herrmann papers, 1910 Box, Baseball Hall of Fame.
8. *Cincinnati Enquirer,* March 7, 1913.
9. *Cincinnati Times-Star,* March 12, 1913.
10. *Cincinnati Enquirer,* March 11, 1913.
11. Telegram, Herrmann Papers, Letters Box, Baseball Hall of Fame.
12. *Cincinnati Enquirer,* March 16, 1913.
13. *Cincinnati Times-Star,* March 13, 1913.
14. *Cincinnati Post,* April 2, 1913.
15. *Cincinnati Times-Star,* February 25, 1913.
16. *Cincinnati Post,* March 25, 1913.
17. *Cincinnati Post,* April 21, 1913.
18. Letter to Herrmann, May 16, 1913, 1910 box, Herrmann Papers, Baseball Hall of Fame.
19. *Cincinnati Tribune,* May 31, 1913.
20. *Cincinnati Enquirer,* May 26, 1913.

21. *Cincinnati Times-Star,* July 11, 1913.
22. *Cincinnati Times-Star,* July 11, 1913.
23. *Cincinnati Enquirer,* July 20, 1913.
24. Letter to Herrmann, 1070 I.J.K box, Herrmann Papers, Baseball Hall of Fame.
25. *Cincinnati Enquirer,* July 24, 1913.
26. *Cincinnati Enquirer,* August 9, 1913.
27. 1910 box, Herrmann Papers, Baseball Hall of Fame.

6. Conflict

1. *Baseball Magazine,* July 15, 1914.
2. *Cincinnati Engquirer,* April 11, 1914.
3. Hailey, p. 66.
4. Rothe, p. 4.
5. Rothe, p. 4.
6. *Cincinnati Enquirer,* April 4, 1914.
7. *Cincinnati Post,* January 22, 1914.
8. *Cincinnati Enquirer,* April 1, 1914.
9. *Cincinnati Enquirer,* April 14, 1914.
10. *Cincinnati Enquirer,* April 14, 1914.
11. *Louisville Courier,* April 4, 1914.
12. *Cincinnati Tribune,* April 4, 1914.
13. *Cincinnati Tribune,* April 6, 1914.
14. *Cincinnati Enquirer,* April 15, 1914.
15. *Cincinnati Tribune,* April 17, 1914.
16. *Cincinnati Tribune,* April 21, 1914.
17. *Cincinnati Tribune,* April 21, 1914.
18. *Cincinnati Enquirer,* April 24, 1914.
19. *Cincinnati Enquirer,* April 21, 1914.
20. *Cincinnati Tribune,* May 13, 1914.
21. *Cincinnati Enquirer,* May 12, 1914.
22. *Cincinnati Enquirer,* June 4, 1914.
23. *Cincinnati Enquirer,* June 4, 1914.
24. *Cincinnati Times-Star,* June 4, 1914.
25. *Cincinnati Enquirer,* June 4, 1914.
26. *Cincinnati Enquirer,* June 6, 1914.
27. *Cincinnati Tribune,* June 1, 1914.
28. *Cincinnati Times-Star,* June 12, 1914.
29. *La Prensa,* June 18, 1914.
30. *Cincinnati Times-Star,* June 25, 1914.
31. *Cincinnati Tribune,* June 4, 1914.
32. *Cincinnati Tribune,* June 4, 1914.
33. *Cincinnati Post,* June 4, 1914.
34. Weir, "The Famous Marsans Case," *Baseball Magazine,* September 1914.
35. *Cincinnati Tribune,* June 5, 1914.
36. *Cincinnati Tribune,* June 5, 1914.
37. *Cincinnati Enquirer,* June 14, 1914.
38. *Cincinnati Times-Star,* June 15, 1914.
39. *Cincinnati Times-Star,* June 17, 1914.

40. *Cincinnati Post,* June 11, 1914.
41. Herrmann Papers, Transfer case 7, Baseball Hall of Fame.
42. *Cincinnati Times-Star,* June 8, 1914.
43. Letter, Herrmann papers, Baseball Hall of Fame.
44. Boas, *Mind of Primitive Man,* p. 125.
45. Boas, *Mind of Primitive Man,* p. 126.
46. Boas, *Mind of Primitive Man,* p. 162.
47. *Cincinnati Times-Star,* June 4, 1914.
48. *St. Louis Dispatch,* June 7, 1914.
49. *Cincinnati Tribune,* June 15, 1914.
50. *Cincinnati Enquirer,* June 9, 1914.
51. *Cincinnati Post,* June 9, 1914.
52. "Marsans to Stick," Jan 11, Marsans file, Baseball Hall of Fame.
53. *St. Louis Star,* June 26, 1914.
54. *Cincinnati Times-Star,* June 12, 1914.
55. Thomas Telegram to Herrmann, Herrmann Papers, Baseball Hall of Fame.
56. Hirschler letter to Marsans, Herrmann Pepers, Baseball Hall of Fame.
57. *La Prensa,* June 13, 1914.
58. *Cincinnati Post,* June 12, 1914.
59. *St. Louis Globe-Democrat,* June 11, 1914.
60. *St. Louis Post-Dispatch,* June 12, 1914.

7. No-Man's Land

1. Untitled, Mordecai Brown clippings file, *The Sporting News.*
2. *Cincinnati Enquirer,* June 14, 1914.
3. *St. Louis Post-Dispatch,* June 14, 1914.
4. *Cincinnati Tribune,* June 15, 1914.
5. *Cincinnati Enquirer,* June 9, 1914.
6. *Cincinnati Enquirer,* June 16, 1914.
7. *Cincinnati Tribune,* June 16, 1914.
8. *La Prensa,* June 17, 1914.
9. *St. Louis Star,* June 17, 1914.
10. *La Prensa,* June 23, 1914
11. *St. Louis Post-Dispatch,* June 25, 1914.
12. *Cincinnati Times-Star,* June 26, 1914.
13. *St. Louis Star,* June 15, 1914.
14. *St. Louis Star,* June 26, 1914.
15. *St. Louis Star,* June 26, 1914.
16. *Cincinnati Enquirer,* June 19, 1914.
17. *St. Louis Globe-Democrat,* June 22, 1914.
18. Marsans Case at St. Louis, p. 44.
19. Marsans Case at St. Louis, p. 3.
20. *Cincinnati Enquirer,* June 23, 1914.
21. *Cincinnati Times-Star,* June 23, 1914.

22. *Cincinnati Post,* July 2, 1914.
23. *La Prensa,* July 6, 1914.
24. *La Prensa,* July 7, 1914.
25. *St. Louis Post-Dispatch,* June 24, 1914.
26. *Sporting News,* July 9, 1914.
27. Letter, Herrmann Papers, Baseball Hall of Fame, 1910 Box.
28. Telegram November 5, 1914, Herrmann Papers, Baseball Hall of Fame.
29. *New York Times,* January 6, 1915.
30. *New York Times,* January 12, 1915.
31. *New York Times,* April 27, 1915.
32. *New York Times,* May 16, 1915.
33. *New York Times,* Jan 1, 1915.
34. *New York Times,* January 24, 1915.
35. *New York Times,* January 30, 1915.
36. *New York Times,* April 10, 1915.
37. *New York Times,* August 10, 1915.
38. *New York Times,* September 23, 1914.
39. *New York Times,* July 13, 1915.
40. *New York Times,* October 16, 1915.
41. Lane, *Baseball Magazine,* May 15, 1915.

8. Resolution

1. "Marsans to Stick" Marsans file, Baseball Hall of Fame.
2. *St. Louis Post-Dispatch,* January 31, 1915.
3. Untitled, Marsans Clipping File, Baseball Hall of Fame.
4. Herrmann Papers, Baseball Hall of Fame.
5. February 18, 1915, Telegram, Herrmann Papers, Baseball Hall of Fame.
6. *St. Louis Star,* March 26, 1915.
7. *St. Louis Globe-Democrat,* March 10, 1915.
8. *St. Louis Republic,* March 9, 1915.
9. *St. Louis Star,* March 9, 1915.
10. *St. Louis Republic,* March 14, 1915.
11. *St. Louis Republic,* March 14, 1915.
12. Commons, p. 7.
13. Commons, p. 128.
14. Fredrickson, p. 101.
15. *St. Louis Globe-Democrat,* March 17, 1915.
16. *St. Louis Globe-Democrat,* March 17, 1915.
17. *St. Louis Star,* March 22, 1915.
18. *St. Louis Star,* March 26, 1915.
19. *St. Louis Globe-Democrat,* March 16, 1915.
20. *St. Louis Globe-Democrat,* March 16, 1915.
21. *St. Louis Globe-Democrat,* April 4, 1915.
22. *St. Louis Star,* April 23, 1915.
23. *St. Louis Star,* May 3, 1915.
24. *St. Louis Post-Dispatch,* May 2, 1915.
25. *St. Louis Post-Dispatch,* June 14, 1915.
26. *St. Louis Post-Dispatch,* May 6, 1915.
27. *St. Louis Post-Dispatch,* June 28, 1915.
28. *St. Louis Post-Dispatch,* August 11, 1915.
29. Marsans Case at St. Louis, p. 41.
30. *Cincinnati Enquirer,* August 17, 1915.
31. *Marsans Case* at St. Louis, p. 28.
32. *New York Times,* August 20, 1915.
33. *New York Times,* August 20, 1915.
34. *St. Louis Post-Dispatch,* August 20, 1915.
35. *St. Louis Post-Dispatch,* August 20, 1915.
36. *St. Louis Star,* August 28, 1915.

9. In the American League

1. Hailey, p. 68.
2. *St. Louis Post-Dispatch,* February 7, 1916.
3. *St. Louis Post-Dispatch,* January 14, 1916.
4. *St. Louis Post-Dispatch,* February 29, 1916.
5. *St. Louis Globe-Democrat,* March 14, 1916.
6. *St. Louis Globe-Democrat,* March 20, 1916.
7. *St. Louis Globe-Democrat,* March 17, 1916.
8. *St. Louis Post-Dispatch,* March 28, 1916.
9. *St. Louis Star,* April 6, 1916.
10. *St. Louis Star,* April 4, 1916.
11. *St. Louis Star,* April 24, 1916.
12. *St. Louis Star,* May 3, 1916.
13. *St. Louis Globe-Democrat,* May 23, 1916.
14. *St. Louis Post-Dispatch,* May 13, 1916.
15. *St. Louis Post-Dispatch,* May 24, 1916.
16. *St. Louis Post-Dispatch,* May 27, 1916.
17. *St. Louis Post-Dispatch,* May 18, 1916.
18. *St. Louis Globe-Democrat,* June 4, 1916.
19. *St. Louis Globe-Democrat,* June 5, 1916.

20. *St. Louis Post-Dispatch*, June 15, 1916.
21. *St. Louis Post-Dispatch*, June 26, 1916,
22. *St. Louis Post-Dispatch*, July 18, 1916.
23. *St. Louis Post-Dispatch*, July 18, 1916.
24. *St. Louis Post-Dispatch*, June 11, 1916.
25. *St. Louis Globe-Democrat*, August 22, 1916.
26. *St. Louis Post-Dispatch*, August 14, 1916.
27. *St. Louis Globe-Democrat*, August 19, 1916.
28. *St. Louis Globe-Democrat*, August 15, 1916.
29. *St. Louis Post-Dispatch*, August 11, 1916.
30. *St. Louis Star*, September 9, 1916.
31. *St. Louis Globe-Democrat*, September 18, 1916.
32. *St. Louis Post-Dispatch*, September 18, 1916.
33. *St. Louis Star*, September 29, 1916.
34. *St. Louis Star*, December 4, 1916.
35. *St. Louis Globe-Democrat*, February 27, 1917.

10. Frustration

1. *St. Louis Star*, March 31, 1917.
2. *St. Louis Star*, April 4, 1917.
3. *St. Louis Globe-Democrat*, March 7, 1917.
4. *St. Louis Post-Dispatch*, March 8, 1917.
5. *St. Louis Star*, April 9, 1917.
6. *St. Louis Globe-Dispatch*, April 7, 1917.
7. *St. Louis Star*, May 17, 1917.
8. *St. Louis Globe-Democrat*, May 30, 1917.
9. *St. Louis Globe-Democrat*, May 22, 1917.
10. *St. Louis Post-Dispatch*, June 10, 1917.
11. *St. Louis Star*, July 16, 1917.
12. *Diario de la Marina*, July 18, 1917.

11. New York

1. *New York American*, March 25, 1918.
2. *New York American*, March 25, 1918.
3. *New York Herald*, March 29, 1918.
4. *New York American*, March 29, 1918.
5. *New York American*, April 8, 1918.
6. *New York American*, March 29, 1918.
7. *New York American*, April 24, 1918.
8. *New York Herald*, April 24, 1918.
9. *New York Herald*, April 25, 1918.
10. *New York Herald*, May 5, 1918.
11. *Diario de la Marina*, May 10, 1918.
12. *New York American*, July 20, 1918.

13. *New York American*, July 20, 1918.
14. *Diario de la Marina*, July 24, 1918.

12. A Belated Return

1. *Louisville Post*, July 11, 1923.
2. *Louisville Post*, July 31, 1923.
3. *Louisville Times*, August 3, 1923.
4. *Cincinnati Times-Star*, August 5, 1923.
5. *Cincinnati Times-Star*, July 22, 1923.
6. *Cincinnati Times-Star*, July 14, 1923.
7. *Cincinnati Post*, August 8, 1923.
8. *Cincinnati Tribune*, August 8, 1923.
9. *Cincinnati Times-Star*, August 8, 1923.
10. *Cincinnati Enquirer*, August 8, 1923.
11. *Louisville Times*, August 9, 1923.
12. *Cincinnati Enquirer*, August 8, 1923.
13. *Cincinnati Post*, August 8, 1923.
14. *Cincinnati Times-Star*, August 10, 1923.
15. *Cincinnati Post*, August 16, 1923.
16. *Sporting News*, August 9, 1923.
17. *Sporting News*, August 9, 1923.
18. *Sporting News*, August 9, 1923.
19. *Louisville Herald*, September 5, 1923.
20. *Sporting News*, September 13, 1923.

13. The Other Side of Segregation

1. González, p. 176.
2. González, p. 271.

14. A Pioneer to the End

1. *Elmira Advertiser*, March 30, 1924.
2. *Elmira Advertiser*, April 4, 1924.
3. *Elmira Advertiser*, April 15, 1924.
4. *Elmira Advertiser*, May 17, 1923.
5. *Elmira Advertiser*, June 4, 1924.
6. *Elmira Advertiser*, June 17, 1924.
7. *Sporting News*, June 12, 1924.
8. *Elmira Advertiser*, June 24, 1924.
9. *Elmira Advertiser*, June 26, 1924.
10. *Elmira Advertiser*, July 29, 1924.
11. *Elmira Advertiser*, July 31, 1924.

15. Game Called

1. Boas, *Mind of Primitive Man*, p. 242.

Bibliography

Baseball Encyclopedia. New York: Macmillan Books.

Benson, Michael. *Ballparks of North America: A Comprehensive Historical Reference to Baseball Grounds, Yards and Stadiums, 1845 to Present.* Jefferson, North Carolina: McFarland, 1989.

Bjarkman, Peter C. *Baseball with a Latin Beat.* Jefferson, North Carolina: McFarland, 1994.

Boas, Franz. *The Mind of Primitive Man.* New York: Macmillan, 1911, 1938.

_____. *Reports of the Immigration Commission, Changes in Bodily Form of Descendants of Immigrants, 61st Congress, Senate.* Washington, D.C.: Washington Government Printing Office, 1911.

Chalmers, David M. *Hooded Americanism: The History of the Ku Klux Klan.* Durham, North Carolina: Duke University Press, 1987.

Commons, John R. *Races and Immigrants in America.* New York: Macmillan, 1907; New York: Kelley, 1938.

Fredrickson, George M. *The Black Image in the White Mind: The Debate on Afro-American Character and Destiny, 1817–1914.* New York: Harper Row, 1971; Middletown, Connecticut: Wesleyan Press, 1987.

Gersham, Michael. *Diamonds: The Evolution of the Ballpark.* New York: Houghton Mifflin Company, 1993.

Giammati, A. Bartlett. *Our Great and Glorious Game.* Chapel Hill, North Carolina: Algonquin, 1998.

Gilbert, Thomas. *Superstars and Monopoly Wars: Nineteenth-Century Major League Baseball.* New York: Franklin Watts, 1995.

González Echevarría, Roberto. *The Pride of Havana: A History of Cuban Baseball.* New York: Oxford University Press, 1999.

Grant, Madison. *The Passing of the Great Race.* New York: Arno, 1918; reprint 1970.

Jacobson, Matthew F. *Barbarian Virtues: The United States Encounters Foreign Peoples at Home and Abroad, 1876–1917.* New York: Hill and Wang, 2000.

Levine, Peter. *Ellis Island to Ebbets Field: Sport and the American Jewish Experience.* New York: Oxford University Press, 1992.

Muro, Raul Diez. *Historia del Base Ball Profesional de Cuba.* Third edition. Cuba: 1949.

Okkonen, Mark. *The Federal League of 1914–1915: Baseball's Third Major League.* Pittsburgh, Pennsylvania: Matthews Publishing, 1989.

Pérez, Louis A. "Between Baseball and Bullfighting: The Quest for Nationality in Cuba," *The Journal of American History,* September 1994.

_____. *Cuba: Between Reform and Revolution.* New York: Oxford University Press, 1995.

Peterson, Robert. *Only the Ball Was White.* Englewood Cliffs, New Jersey: Prentice Hall, 1970; revised edition. New York: Oxford University Press, 1992.

Phelon, W.M. "Baseball in Cuba," *The Baseball Magazine.*

Ross, Edward Alsworth. *The Old World in the New: The Significance of Past and Present Immigration to the American People.* New York: The Century Company, 1913.

Rothe, Emil. "Was the Federal League a Major League?" *Baseball Research Journal,* 1981. Society for American Baseball Research, Cooperstown. 1981.

Newspapers

Cincinnati Enquirer, Cincinnati, Ohio
Cincinnati Post, Cincinnati, Ohio
Cincinnati Times-Star, Cincinnati, Ohio
Cincinnati Tribune, Cincinnati, Ohio
Diario de la Marina, Havana, Cuba
Elmira Advertiser, Elmira, New York
Holyoke Daily Tribune, Holyoke, Massachusetts
La Lucha, Havana, Cuba
La Prensa, Havana, Cuba
Louisville Courier, Louisville, Kentucky
Louisville Courier-Journal, Louisville, Kentucky
Louisville Herald, Louisville, Kentucky
Louisville Post, Louisville, Kentucky
Louisville Times, Louisville, Kentucky
New Britain Herald, New Britain, Connecticut
New Britain Record, New Britain, Connecticut
New York American, New York, New York
New York Herald, New York, New York
New York Times, New York, New York

Sporting Life
Sporting News
Springfield Union, Springfield, Massachusetts
Stamford Daily Advocate, Stamford, Connecticut
St. Louis Post-Dispatch, St. Louis, Missouri
St. Louis Globe-Democrat, St. Louis, Missouri
St. Louis Republic, St. Louis, Missouri
St. Louis Star, St. Louis, Missouri

Clippings Files

Armando Marsans File, National Baseball Hall of Fame, Cooperstown, N.Y.
Joe Tinker File, National Baseball Hall of Fame, Cooperstown, N.Y.
Mordecai Brown Clippings File, *Sporting News,* St. Louis, Missouri

Documents

August Herrmann Papers, National Baseball Hall of Fame, Cooperstown, N.Y.
Marsans Case at St. Louis, Organized Baseball

Index

185